THE
BLIFFEN
FAMILY

A Legacy of Faith

THE
BLIFFEN
FAMILY

A Legacy of Faith

JERRY D. BLIFFEN

XULON PRESS

Xulon Press
2301 Lucien Way #415
Maitland, FL 32751
407.339.4217
www.xulonpress.com

ISBN-13: 978-1-6628-4313-6

TABLE OF CONTENTS

PROLOGUE

It was a Sunday morning in the late 1930s, near the end of the Great Depression, when Ralph and Aleta Bliffen, with their six children (three were not yet born), attended Sixth Avenue Church of Christ in Huntington, West Virginia. A young lad, Charles Ballard, attended church with the Bliffen family, and on this particular Sunday he was surprised when the offering was received. No one had a lot of money, especially this family of eight! But when the offering tray was passed, Ralph Bliffen put in a $20 bill for the Lord's work. Young Charles had never even seen a $20 bill and needless to say, this one unselfish act of giving made a lasting impression on him. I'm thankful to say Ralph was my Grandfather, and Charles later became a fellow preacher of the gospel. In his golden years, Charles became a member of the Coal Run Church of Christ, where I ministered. Charles was one of many, like Bill Morgan and nine Bliffen children, who attended Kentucky Christian College in the 1940s, 50s, and 60s from the Sixth Avenue Church of Christ in Huntington, West Virginia. In fact, at least 38 young people from that church attended Kentucky Christian College, many of whom went into the Christian ministry. It's interesting to note that at least one "Bliffen" was on the campus of Kentucky Christian College for 30 consecutive years, 1947-1977. How sad it is that the Sixth Avenue Church of Christ, so instrumental in the shaping of lives of many for Christian service, exists no more, and the building now sits empty adjacent to the Marshall University campus.

The Bliffen family is unique ... we rejoice in a wonderful "Legacy of Faith." Our story is the true account of what God can do through people who are committed to Him, His Son Jesus Christ, and the Kingdom of God.

The information within these pages has come to me from many sources, primarily family members. I am grateful to all who have shared our family story and hope those who read it will be inspired to serve the Lord as long as they live. Special thanks to my wife, Sheila who has worked many hours to help make this book possible.

The following chapters will be dedicated to briefly tell of the lives and ministries of my grandparents, their nine children, as well as my immediate family and myself. Also included is a chapter devoted to the life and ministry of my father-in-law, E.W. Damron. Several family members assisted in producing this work by submitting their own stories which are noted at the beginning of each chapter. Finally, I have included a brief history of the Vansant Church of Christ and the Coal Run Church of Christ, the churches I served for many years.

God's providential work in our lives to advance His Kingdom, both in our nation and around the world, is evident on every page. However, this book is not to glorify our family, but to glorify the God and Father of our family! Many Bliffens have chosen to take the Great Commission seriously: "Therefore, go and make disciples of all nations, baptizing them in the name of the Father, and of the Son, and of the Holy Spirit, and teaching them to obey everything I have commanded you. And surely, I am with you always, to the very end of the age." (Matthew 28:19-20 NIV.) Heaven will surely be a marvelous family reunion for us and the host of others our family has helped to win and disciple for Jesus Christ!

LEGACY OF FAITH
BY JOHN DEAN BLIFFEN, 2000

My grandmas and grandpas
raised their families in the hard times.
Though they never had riches, God provided all their needs.
They took their children to church
where they learned about Jesus.
And all through their lives, they passed down a living faith.
They believed in family values, they were faithful to the Lord,
And they gave to their children the greatest gift,
worth much more than pure gold.

They left a legacy of faith, an inheritance of service.
They taught their children to love the Lord
and to serve him all their lives.
From generation to generation,
a living faith has been passed down.
And now as we teach our children, we leave a legacy of faith.

In ten states and in Rhodesia, their children all served the Lord,
And now the next generation extends that service even more.
There was no family business and no wealth to be passed down,
But the riches of God's grace
have been preached throughout the world.
They believed in family values, they were faithful to the Lord,
And they gave to their children the greatest gift,
worth much more than pure gold.

They left a legacy of faith, an inheritance of service.
They taught their children to love the Lord
and to serve him all their lives.
From generation to generation,
a living faith has been passed down.
And now as we teach our children, we leave a legacy of faith.

Ralph and Aleta Bliffen

Chapter 1

Ralph and Aleta Bliffen
By Jack, Jerry and Aleta Bliffen

My Grandfather, Ralph Dalton Bliffen, was born in Greenbrier County, West Virginia on April 21, 1904 to Christopher Roadcap and Rose Bliffen. Ralph had two brothers: Theodore (Ted) Roosevelt and Robert Dennis, and one sister, Zella. When Ralph was a teenager, the family moved to Huntington, West Virginia. He worked as a projectionist at a movie theater, where he met his future wife, Aleta and they were married May 22, 1926. Ralph was employed as a linotype operator at Standard Printing & Publishing Company in Huntington. This job required him to prepare the typeface for the printing machines, which involved creating a form of lead type. This form weighed about 450 pounds which he had to move to the presses. It was a very physically demanding occupation.

Early in his life, Ralph had been diagnosed with tuberculosis and was told that he would not live to more than 20 years of age. This motivated him to do what he could to promote a healthy body that would prove the doctor wrong. Thus, he became a follower of Charles Atlas, the famous weightlifter. It was through the Atlas exercise program that he developed an impressive physique. We are blessed to have many pictures of Ralph's muscular body that can be found on the Facebook page "Bliffen Stories."

Ralph was raised in the Lutheran faith, and Aleta was a Methodist. After they started their family, they decided to go to only one church together.

Ralph determined to read the Bible and find the church whose teachings were the closest to the Bible teachings. As providence would have it, someone invited Aleta to the Sixth Avenue Church of Christ in Huntington. She soon realized that this was the church they had been looking for. When she told Ralph about it, he said, "I'll see." After attending 3 months, they were baptized into Christ, attended faithfully and raised their family in the Church of Christ.

Through the years, Ralph continued to improve his body. He eventually became a semi-professional wrestler and weight-lifting performer. He has been pictured holding a 400-pound barbell and in another picture holding a 190-pound barbell over his head with one arm. As a wrestler, he used the name "The Masked Marvel" and traveled as far as Columbus, Ohio to wrestle. His good friend and often competitor Harry Steinborn, used the name "Milo" from the 6th Century BC Greek wrestler, "Milo of Croton." (My Dad, Jack's middle name came from Harry Steinborn's wrestling name, Jack "Milo" Bliffen.) Ralph's wrestling career ended the day the promoters told him who was supposed to win the match. Obviously, he didn't intend on losing any matches! He also knew this was dishonest, and as a Christian he would have no part in it.

My grandparents moved to Tampa, Florida in 1960, when Granddad was 56 years old. When they moved, he rode his motorcycle from Huntington to Tampa, long before there were interstate highways. About half-way there, he encountered motor trouble with his motorcycle and was only able to travel at 30 miles an hour for the remainder of the trip!

Being too young to begin drawing his retirement pay, Ralph took a job with the Tampa Tribune where he worked for a few years. It was common to see him riding his Harley wearing his captain's hat (no helmet) to work. Being a printer, Ralph took advantage of the opportunity to publish his own book. He titled it, "What I Know About Birth Control" by Ralph D. Bliffen. Being a father of nine, it was full of empty pages! He probably knew it wouldn't sell very well as he only produced one copy! When visiting my grandparents as a boy in Tampa, I remember my grandfather still lifting weights and tanning in the middle of the summer in his back yard. He maintained his healthy body as long as he lived.

On November 17,1967, Granddad's earthly journey ended when he suffered a massive stroke at the age of 63. The day before his death he used an ax to cut down a good-sized tree. Granddad was a strong man and had a great sense of humor. But his greatest strength was his commitment to the Lord and to his family.

Aleta Watrous, my Grandmother, was born on a farm, near Gallipolis, Ohio on September 27, 1908. As a young woman she would cross the Ohio River and attend movies in Huntington, where she met and later married "the projectionist," Ralph. Aleta went to the hospital to give birth to her first child, Marie, but was totally unhappy with that experience. She decided never to go back to the hospital again to give birth, so her other eight children were born at home! Aleta was an amazing shopper and cook, providing meals for her ever-growing family. She also was a talented seamstress, making clothes for her entire family.

When the children were young, every New Year's Eve the Bliffens hosted a party for the youth of the Sixth Avenue Church. The church would have a service that would last until midnight and then all of the young people would go the Bliffens' home. The party would last all night. It grew in attendance to over 100 different people coming and going throughout the night. On one occasion, Aleta fed breakfast to over 60 people. One New Years' Eve, in order to economically feed more people, she invented "Bliffen Burgers." A "Bliffen Burger" is one half of a hamburger bun, spread thinly with a mixture of hamburger meat, onion, salt, egg, ketchup and sometimes breadcrumbs, then broiled in an oven. "Bliffen Burgers" have become a family tradition and have been served around the world by family and friends.

(The next section of text was written by my Grandma, Aleta. Thanks to Erin Bliffen Simpson for sharing it.)

My Junior year of high school I met Ralph Bliffen at Kathleen's house. I really liked him. Soon he got a bad sore throat, so I called on the phone to find out how he was. After he got out again, he asked me to the show (movie) with him and that was in November. For Christmas that year he got me a gold watch. I was really happy with that. We always went to the show and then to the ice cream parlor for ice cream. One night he took me to the place where his sister Zella worked. She was the first one of his family I had met. He had a Sterns Knight touring car. He also had a motorcycle. He came by one day and I went out and talked to him and my Dad didn't know him and didn't approve of that at all. I was so interested in Ralph my grades were (I thought) slipping. We got engaged in about March and I just knew I would flunk all my classes. So, I said I wanted to get married before school was out so they could write withdrawal on my card. Instead of bad cards they all gave me good grades except for my English teacher, and she didn't like me anyway (at least that is what I thought) so she didn't grade me, I don't think. Anyway, we got married May 22, 1926.

Ralph always treated me like I was someone special. I guess I thought he was very special too. He went to the Lutheran Church Bible School. He went pretty regular but missed a week or so. They wrote a card about one bad apple in a barrel so he never went back. I went to the Methodist Church. I had been sprinkled at a revival when I was 12 years old. I thought baptism was of no matter. I attended a Christian Church at an invitation from a friend, Louise Myers. There, the Bible class under Hester Green started reading the New Testament and after 3 months I knew I needed to be immersed into Christ, so that Wednesday evening Ms. Jacobs and I were baptized. While we were dressing, Preacher Ingram read the 6th chapter of Romans. So, the next Sunday evening Ralph went forward and was immersed into Christ. Always from then on, we each read our Bibles and tried to live by what we read. We had Marie, Jack and Betty by this time.

Soon after we were married Ralph started lifting weights. He had a lot of self-discipline and never missed working with the weights every other night. He also wrestled professionally until we were converted. Then he quit, he thought it was wrong. He had wrestled in Columbus, Ohio and Logan, West Virginia.

When Jack was a baby, we built a living room across the front of our house and a bath on the back. After 6 children we decided the house was just too small and we had to find a larger house. We looked all over Huntington. Anything we wanted cost too much. Anything we could afford was in a bad neighborhood. There was a big old farmhouse across the street. Finally, it was put up for sale, and we bought it. It was in bad condition, but we worked on it and lived in it 20 years. We had 3 more children over there, making 9.

After Marie and Jack were in high school, we had a party every Sunday evening from 9:00-10:00 PM for the young people and once a year we had an all-night New Year's Eve party. Usually, 35 stayed for breakfast. About 75 came through most of the night. No one under 15 could come. When we moved to Florida, some of the 15-year-old children thought that wasn't fair, they had waited all their lives and then we moved.

I used to go to the market once a week and buy fruits and vegetables. I used to can a lot. I also made nearly all the clothes the children wore. Most of the coats were made from hand-me-downs. I would rip a coat apart and wash and press the material, then make a coat for whoever needed it. That way our children were always well dressed. As they got older and worked some, they helped and bought coats, jackets, shoes, etc.

We always had a car, comfortable house and good food on the table. After Ralph and I became Christians we tithed all our money and the Lord blessed us. We never missed church except when sick or two times the ice and snow were so bad, we couldn't get there.

Everyone told me I over protected my children, but I never thought it was necessary for them to fall into sin to know it was wrong. So, I tried to keep them away from sin. I taught them good ways to have fun. There was almost always a game of some kind going at our house. I thought that was a lot better than quarreling and fighting, so they learned how to treat each other.

Ralph didn't argue or fuss. He followed the Bible. His yea was yea, and nay was nay. I still think that is what God had in mind for us. I could always trust Ralph's answers, they never seemed to be wrong. I always kept him informed so he knew all the background. We always talked over what went on that day at night before we went to sleep.

How blessed we are to have Grandma's story in her own words!

After Granddad's death, Grandma Aleta studied typing in order to become a church secretary. She served in this capacity for the Westshore Christian Church in Tampa. She was also a Sunday School teacher. Her daughter, Mary, a missionary in Rhodesia, (now Zimbabwe) Africa, recruited her to go to Africa and work as a House Mother at the Bible College that was founded by John Pemberton and Dennis Pruett. In Africa, Grandma served as the Director of Housekeeping for the Mashoko Hospital in Hippo Valley, 100 miles from the nearest city. Grandma Aleta's African mission work continued for three years. After her return to the states, she lived alone in Tampa as long as she was able. When her health deteriorated to the point that it was no longer good for her to live independently, she went to live with Mary, who by this time was working at Cookson Hills Children's Home in Kansas, Oklahoma. Grandma Aleta died in Oklahoma from a bleeding ulcer on August 14, 1988, about a month before her 80th birthday. At her death, my Dad, Jack, borrowed a van, drove from Eustis, Florida to Oklahoma, picked up Grandma's body and brought it to Huntington, West Virginia where her memorial service was held, appropriately at the Sixth Avenue Church of Christ. She is buried beside her husband in the Ridgelawn Memorial Park Cemetery in Huntington.

My grandparents were opposites in many ways. Granddad was quiet and not at all outgoing. He did not attend Sunday school because he feared he might be called on to publicly pray or answer a teacher's question. Yet his character was squeaky clean. In fact, he even earned the nickname, "Mr. Clean." And yes, he did physically resemble "Mr. Clean" as well. Grandma was very outgoing and personable. When we visited, Grandma loved to play cards ... especially a card game called "canasta." Everyone who ever played with her knows she always played to win, even if it meant fooling her granddaughter, Jane! Playing cards has always been a Bliffen tradition. I think it is fair to say that most of the Bliffens inherited the personality of Grandma and possessed the integrity of both Grandma and Granddad.

When one considers the children and grandchildren of Ralph and Aleta, you know they were a remarkable couple, the epitome of successful Christian parents. Today they enjoy the reward of lives lived for the Lord in their heavenly home and we all look forward to a great reunion in Glory!

Ralph

Aleta

Bliffen Family

Bliffen Siblings
Row 1: Peggy, Mary, Betty, Marie
Row 2: Joe, John, Steve, Jerry, Jack

Marie and daughters
Row1: Rose Anne, Karen Lou, Marie
Row 2: Sallie Jo, Linda

Chapter 2

HELEN MARIE AND JOHN STUMBO

By Sallie Jo Nickell and Jerry Bliffen

Helen Marie Bliffen was the first of nine children born to Ralph and Aleta on September 1, 1927. They were all born and raised in Huntington, West Virginia and became members of the Sixth Avenue Church of Christ. Marie told her children this story, that as she and her siblings grew up, they slept upstairs with a window slightly open, even on the coldest nights. Because they had open fireplaces downstairs, Grandma Bliffen wanted her children to sleep upstairs away from the fires. Marie said many mornings they awoke with snow on their blankets and on the floor beside their bed.

Marie met John Hermon Stumbo at Kentucky Christian College, where they were students. They married in 1949 at the Sixth Avenue Church of Christ and lived in a small log cabin on the campus of Kentucky Christian College as they continued their education. After they both graduated, John accepted his first full-time ministry at Ravenna, Kentucky. Sallie Jo shared, "Dad had such a personality that he struck up a rapport with a number of the church members. He was in wide demand for revivals and traveled extensively. Leaving Kentucky, he accepted a preaching ministry at Okolona, Mississippi. From there he moved to Kosciusko, Mississippi."

"Mom and Dad's marriage was blessed with four girls: Linda Marie, Sallie Jo, Rose Anne, and Karen Lou. They moved to Liberty, Kentucky in 1955 where Dad preached until 1962. Our family then moved *east*, from Liberty to West Liberty, Kentucky (a Kentucky wonder!) where Dad became the minister of the West Liberty Christian Church on November 27, 1962. After about a year ministering in West Liberty, Dad fell on our back steps and broke his upper back. He had previously broken his back in the same place while serving our country overseas in WW II, which made this accident fatal. He died later that same evening at the age of 37. President Kennedy had been assassinated just a few days before, and Dad had conducted a memorial service in the public school for grades 5-12 in which he played some audio recordings of John Kennedy's speeches. The community was impressed with how profound that service was. Then Mom unexpectedly had to plan a funeral for her beloved John."

"Mother became a widow at the young age of 36 with four young girls to raise by herself. At that time Linda was 13, I was 11, Rose Anne was 9, and Karen Lou was 8. Mother, a veteran's widow, worked hard to collect educational benefits for her daughters. She had graduated from Kentucky Christian College, but the state would not recognize her degree. Mom had been a homemaker her entire marriage, so in order to find employment that would sustain our family, she enrolled at Morehead State University for a one-year program to become a Social Worker. She became employed by the state of Kentucky in Morgan County. Mother received the proceeds of a small life insurance policy after Dad's death, which allowed her to purchase materials for a brick house. Yet being the ever-faithful servant of Christ, she tithed of even that life insurance payment in faith that the Lord would provide. At this time her oldest brother, Jack, was employed at Kentucky Christian College in nearby Grayson, Kentucky. He took the responsibility of building a house for Mom and our family. Other men of the family helped as they were able. Her youngest brother Joe was attending KCC at that time, so he and his friends provided much needed volunteer labor."

"For a while, Uncle Jack preached at the West Liberty Christian Church after Daddy's death. Joe Nevius became the next full-time minister, retiring around 1969. Uncle Steve Bliffen then came to minister to West Liberty

Christian where he served for 30 years until his death in 1999. On one occasion after Steve moved to West Liberty, our cousin Jane, Jack's daughter, came over from KCC to spend the weekend with us. Steve had just bought a new car and he volunteered to allow Mom to use it to drive Jane back to Grayson on Sunday night. My husband, Phillip, and I went along as company for Mom. As she was driving along a little too fast, she bumped the side of a bridge and declared, 'I think I bumped that bridge.' She didn't even stop! I couldn't believe it."

"After Daddy died, money was always scarce. We had four girls in school wearing pantyhose every day, because we were not allowed to wear pants to school. I always had to wear hand-me-down clothes from Linda until I grew taller than her. Then Mother made my clothes! I do remember going to a store one time in my life to pick out a top and a pair of shorts. Everything else was handmade by my Mom. We never had store-bought formals. Each one was lovingly made by Mother's hands. I still have the velveteen dress Mom made for my wedding day, and Grandma Bliffen hand embroidered the bodice."

"Every payday Mother allowed each of us girls to buy one 16 oz. Pepsi. That was our allotment for the month! As a social worker, she was a child advocate. She had clients with children who had to bring in coal every day to heat their houses. They didn't have gloves and their hands would split open and bleed. She would take money out of her own meager pocket and buy Dial soap and Jergen's lotion for the children's hands. She once said that her job was not for a married person because if you were devoted to it like you should be, you didn't have time for a spouse.'"

"Mother was diagnosed with breast cancer in 1976. She faced her struggle with that horrible disease bravely and with a strong faith. I accompanied her to most of her appointments at the UK Medical Center for radiation. As we would sit in the waiting room, several bald-headed children would be around us, and Mom would look at me with tears in her eyes and say, 'You know, no matter how bad of a shape you get in, you can always look around and see someone in worse shape.' Mother went to be with the Lord on June 29, 1977 at the age of 49. Later my sister, Linda, also died of breast cancer in 2000 at the age of 49. Life can be hard at times, but God is always good!"

Jack and family
Jack, Jean, John, Jerry, Jane, Jim

Chapter 3

JACK MILO AND JEAN BLIFFEN
BY JACK AND JERRY BLIFFEN

I t was October 7, 1929 when Ralph and Aleta Bliffen welcomed their second child, my Dad, Jack Milo Bliffen, into the world in Huntington, West Virginia. Ohio Avenue, Huntington was where the Bliffen homeplace was located and where the nine Bliffen children were raised. The first of five sons, Dad was named for two of his Father's heroes, Jack Dempsey, a world champion boxer, and Harry "Milo" Steinberg, a semi- professional wrestler who used the stage name "Milo" from the great 6th century B.C. Greek wrestler.

The Bliffens were a very devout Christian family and members of the Sixth Avenue Church of Christ. From the age of two weeks Dad was taken to church. As the family grew, Ralph and Aleta saw to it that their children were faithful in church attendance. Dad was baptized at the age of 8 and later ordained to the ministry at the age of 19. My dad had a happy childhood in Huntington and graduated from Huntington East High School before entering Kentucky Christian College in 1947. During his college years, Dad worked one summer as a lifeguard for the Dreamland Swimming Pool in Kenova...one of the largest swimming pools in West Virginia. Interestingly, many years later, I married the granddaughter of a man who helped construct that pool, Jerome Damron. Dad also worked summer jobs at a Cadillac dealer and Jimmy's Steak House in Huntington.

The first sermon he ever preached was at the Antioch Christian Church in Phil, Kentucky, near Liberty, on October 10, 1947. That church was being served by a fellow student and friend, Denny Pruett, a man who would later help begin Central Africa Christian Mission, and become a medical doctor. The trip from Grayson to Phil was an 8-hour drive, which they made on Saturday. Dad's sermon was only 7 minutes long! They then had to drive eight hours back to the college on Sunday afternoon. His second sermon was at the Brush Creek Christian Church, which was also near Liberty. It was in 1948, during his college years that Dad accepted a weekend ministry at the Coal Run Church of Christ in Pikeville, Kentucky. Coal Run is the church I later served as full-time minister for 30 years. Coincidentally, my father-in-law, E.W. Damron, was their first full-time minister and served at Coal Run for 29 years. In 1950-51 Dad was an Intern Associate Minister at the Guyandotte Christian Church on the outskirts of Huntington. Also, while a college student, he preached revivals at Olive Branch, Kentucky, Westmoreland, West Virginia, Russell, Kentucky, Brownstown, Indiana, and his home church in Huntington. He actually baptized both of his youngest brothers, John and Joe, in that revival meeting!

In 1945, Dad met his forever sweetheart, Carolyn Jean Fultz, at summer Christian camp on the campus of Kentucky Christian College. Mom lived in Charleston, West Virginia, the daughter of Charles David and Yolanda Fultz. Because Dad had no automobile, he would hitchhike a ride to Charleston and take his sweetie roller skating, then hitchhike back to Huntington. Years later, Dad and Mom could still skate circles around people half their age!

Mom's parents, Charles & Yolanda Fultz were faithful Christians. In fact, my Grandpa Fultz was an elder and supply preacher in different churches around Charleston as well as the organist for the South Boulevard Church of Christ. Grandpa actually played the organ at the funeral service for the mother of his favorite preacher, Clarence Greenleaf, in 1955. Greenleaf's deceased mother was a Hatfield related to the feuding Hatfield's from the Hatfield/McCoy Feud. Fast forward 21 years, and Clarence Greenleaf became a good friend of mine and mentored me in the ministry. Grandpa Fultz was employed as the Chief Payroll Officer for Southeastern Greyhound

18

Lines. Mom had one older sister, Joan, who married U.S. Lester, both of whom were students at Kentucky Christian College. She also had a younger brother, David, who served in the United States Navy, and then attended Cincinnati Bible Seminary before going into the ministry.

On December 18, 1950, Dad married his sweetheart, Carolyn Jean Fultz. In the spring of 1951, Dad graduated from Kentucky Christian College. After graduation, his first full time ministry was at Eskdale Church of Christ in West Virginia, located about halfway between Charleston and Beckley. He ministered there in 1951-1952. It was while serving there that Mom gave birth to their first child, Carol Jane on January 10, 1952. Later that year they moved to Bethesda, Ohio, where Dad preached for the South Main Street Church of Christ until 1955. While living in Bethesda, their family grew as Mom gave birth to two sons, Jerry David (me) on April 11, 1954, and James Daniel, on August 2, 1955. My parents had originally planned to name me "Steve" after one of Dad's brothers but because I was born on my Uncle Jerry Harrison's birthday, I was named "Jerry." My middle name, David, came from Mom's father, Charles David and her brother, David. James or "Jim" was named for Dad's youngest brother, James Joseph, better known as "Joe."

Dad has always been a lover of learning, so in 1955 our family moved to Pittsburg, Pennsylvania so he could enroll in the University of Pittsburgh to pursue a Master of Education degree. While living in Pittsburgh, Dad ministered to the First Christian Church in Braddock, Pennsylvania from 1955-1958. After completing his master's degree in 1958, Dad and Mom packed up and moved again to Vanceburg, Kentucky where Dad preached for the First Christian Church until 1961. It was while we lived in Vanceburg that our family became complete when Mom gave birth to my little brother, John Dean, on October 30, 1959, in Portsmouth, Ohio. In keeping with the family tradition, John was also named for two of Dad's younger brothers, John Hamilton and Stephen Dean.

In 1959, Dad became employed as Professor and Business Manager at his alma mater, Kentucky Christian College. He later became Vice President in 1965. Our family of six moved to Grayson, Kentucky around 1960, but Dad continued for a while to drive on Sundays to Vanceburg to preach. After his brother-in-law in West Liberty, preacher John Stumbo, died suddenly in 1963, Dad filled the pulpit at the West Liberty Christian Church in 1964. While serving the college full time throughout the 60's, he also held part-time ministries at the Carter City Christian Church in 1964 – 65, and the Oak Grove Church of Christ from 1966 - 69. It was while preaching at Carter City that a generous elder and local merchant, J.F. Lewis, would occasionally fill the Bliffen station wagon with many bags of groceries. Our family would eat very well for over a week! Dad became well acquainted with the curvy roads in the foothills of the Bluegrass State preaching some-where almost every Sunday, all the while being a full-time Professor and Business Manager for a Bible College that was training preachers to go out and preach the gospel. When he would travel to recruit students for the college, he would always ask the churches to send their "very best" young people to train for the ministry. The college did not exist as a reform school. It was a school whose primary task was the training of preachers for the evan-gelism of the world! While living in Grayson, he also found time to further his education, taking classes at the University of Kentucky where he earned a certificate of College Business Management.

When his older sister in West Liberty was left widowed with a family of 4 girls to raise, Dad made time to help build a house for Marie. He later built a house for our family in the Green Acres subdivision of Grayson. Dad could do almost anything if it involved construction! I enjoyed living at Green Acres, mainly because the Little Sandy River was behind our backyard! We had the perfect swimming hole, which we took advantage of on many hot summer days! Dad even helped construct the Kentucky Christian College library on College Street, where later his own children would spend hours in research, writing many term papers. In 1966 Dad was instrumental in helping Professor Don Nash's son, Francis, get a job at WGOH radio sta-tion. Once Francis was hired there, he continued to work for that radio sta-tion for 50 years, retiring recently as the General Manager! Dad's work and influence on the campus of Kentucky Christian College and in the lives of many he touched while employed there still live on today.

In the summer of 1969, our family moved yet again to Atlanta Georgia, where Dad became Vice President of Atlanta Christian College. This was a traumatic move for us boys. Jane had enrolled at Kentucky Christian College that fall, but Jim, John and I had to start new schools in Atlanta. It was truly culture shock for us. But we adjusted, and Dad served the college until 1971. While there he was also a part-time minister for the Central Christian Church in Atlanta. In 1972, Dad left Atlanta Christian College to become the Business Manager for Christian City, an orphanage and retirement community located southwest of Atlanta. This was a short-lived employment as in December of 1972, we again moved, this time to Johnson City, Tennessee, where Dad became the Minister of the Downtown Christian Church. I had started college at Kentucky Christian College that fall, having left Atlanta for Grayson. But at Christmas break, I had to go "home," not to Atlanta, but to Johnson City, where I had never lived. I later jokingly said, "They moved a lot, but I always found them!"

In 1975, Dad accepted an invitation to become President of Mid-South Christian College in Senatobia, Mississippi, where he served until 1980. He was thrilled for the opportunity, and this was a very fulfilling ministry for him, but also very stressful as he had to be a Professor, Business Manager, Dean, Fundraiser, and Student Recruiter for a small Bible College in a part of the country where Christian Churches were few and far between. Some of that time he also served as a part time minister for the First Christian Church in Millington, Tennessee. My youngest brother, John, was a student at Mid-South Christian during Dad's tenure there and my brother, Jim, became Student Recruiter for the college. Both brothers and our cousin Tom Thomas sang in a very popular quartet among the mid-south churches called "Tribute." They traveled representing the college and were very successful in recruiting students for Mid-South Christian College. While attending school and traveling as recruiters, God led Jim and John to the girls He had picked for their mates. Jim's wife, Joni, was from Arkansas, and John's wife, Becky, was from Mississippi. What a blessing these ladies have been to my brothers in their ministries.

After much success in building up Mid-South Christian College, Dad and Mom, now empty nesters, moved to Clearwater, Florida in 1980 where he worked with a unique ministry, "Project Look Up". This ministry was in conjunction with Good News Productions International, founded by Ziden Nutt, and was a mission finding means to utilize satellites in proclaiming the gospel in various countries around the world. This work has expanded to reach millions of people around the world. While working with this ministry he also preached for First Christian Church in Crystal River, Florida until 1981.

In 1983, Dad answered the call to minister to First Church of Christ in Eustis, Florida. This congregation was steeped in restoration history, being founded by W.K. Pendleton, son-in-law of Alexander Campbell, in the late 1800s. Dad had a good ministry in Eustis and made many good friends in that church. The church's name was later changed to Lake Eustis Christian Church during my brother-in-law, Bob Bender's ministry there. While preaching in Eustis, Dad also started The Florida Bible Conference, which is an ongoing ministry now under the direction of the Christian Restoration Association. It is a three-day conference in January, presently meeting at the Kissimmee Christian Church. Dad served as the chairman of the Bible Conference from 1990-2012.

After his ministry in Eustis, Dad and Mom moved to Pompano Beach, where he worked with Florida Haitian Christian Mission from 1991-1996. During this ministry Dad helped the Haitian brethren establish churches in several locations in southern Florida. Most of these churches continue to thrive in evangelizing the Haitian people in Florida. Our Haitian brethren still have a high regard for my Dad and appreciate the work he did to help them establish their congregations.

Preaching and teaching the gospel were always Dad's first love, so in 1996, he became the minister of the First Christian Church in Cocoa Beach. We were glad he was there because they lived only four blocks from the beach! While ministering in Cocoa Beach, Dad learned of the need to start a new congregation in the nearby city of Viera, where there was no Christian Church. So, in 2001, Dad and Mom and a few other Christian couples helped launch the

Viera Christian Church just north of Melbourne. Around that time Dad and Mom moved into a retirement community in Rockledge, Florida. The church in Viera met with a lot of obstacles: finances, government red tape, building codes and other regulations that prevented them from building in the city of Viera. Eventually the church decided to relocate on US 1 in the nearby community of Palm Shores. The name of the church became "The Christian Church at Palm Shores" and is presently served by evangelist Greg Dill. Dad preached for this church from 2001 until 2014. At the age of 85, Dad finally retired, and he and Mom moved into an apartment in his daughter Jane's home in Umatilla, Florida, just north of Eustis. But God was not finished with Dad yet! He was soon called to preach for the Yalaha Community Church, a small congregation that is about 150 years old. Yalaha is a small, picturesque community on Lake Harris about 14 miles from Eustis. Dad has thoroughly enjoyed his ministry to the people of "the little white church by the lake." He has baptized some people into Christ, preached and taught the word of God, and observed the Lord's supper every Sunday in their 6:00 PM service. He has been a tremendous blessing to the Yalaha Community Church, and the ministry there has been a huge blessing to my Dad.

My parents enjoyed a happy marriage for over 68 years, but on September 28, 2019, my sweet Mother went home to be with the Lord at the age of 89. Mom was by Dad's side and supportive of his ever-changing ministries through all the years of their marriage. Her primary work was a homemaker and mother, though she did teach kindergarten and sold Avon products during part of the time we lived in Grayson. Having a beautiful voice, Mom sang solos in church, sang in church choirs, and led congregational singing in several different congregations through the years. Dad and Mom's love for each other was great and evident. Dad was able to demonstrate just how great his love for Mom was as her health declined and she suffered from dementia. I admired how Dad cared for Mom in her final chapter of life, and when she passed, he said, "There's nothing wrong with going to heaven." Mom's remains have been placed in the church yard at the Lake Eustis Christian Church. Just recently, Dad, at 91 years old, was invited to preach for the Sugar Grove Christian Church, near Mt. Sterling, Kentucky, where Francis Nash has ministered for 53 years, since a student at Kentucky Christian College. There were 26 Bliffen family members in service that morning, and what a great gospel message we heard from my Dad! At this writing, Dad is 92 years old, and is still teaching Bible classes at Eustis and Yalaha on Tuesdays and Wednesdays in addition to preaching on Sunday evenings at Yalaha Community Church. He has been involved in some variety of ministry for 72 years, in 7 different states! However, he loves Florida and has no plans to drive in the snow ever again! Through the years, Dad has taken many short-term mission trips to other countries. He has been to Thailand, Burma, Grenada, Haiti (5 times), Cuba (3 times), Jamaica (twice) and Uruguay. One time in Jamaica the natives cooked a goat for their visitors and gave Dad a cup full of meat with the goat's eyes on the top of his cup. Unfortunately, the eyes "fell" out of the cup onto the ground before he could eat them! My mother was also blessed to travel with Dad on some of those trips. Knowing that the gospel of Jesus Christ is the only hope for a lost and dying world, Dad was happy to be able to experience these short-term mission opportunities, sometimes teaching, sometimes doing construction work, and sometimes being a support person for his youngest son on the mission field.

My Dad is extremely intelligent! For much of his life he worked the crossword puzzle in the newspaper almost every morning. He probably never lost a game of Scrabble or Chess. He has lost a few card games, though it was only because he had a bad hand dealt to him or a weak partner. He still enjoys playing cards with anyone willing to play! He continues to preach excellent sermons without any notes. His favorite quote from another preacher is: "I love you, and there's nothing you can do about it." His favorite song and theological thought: "Jesus loves me, this I know, for the Bible tells me so."

Dad's multi-faceted ministry is an amazing example of what God can do with a man totally committed to the greatest work on earth! Mom's life is equally an example of unselfish love and commitment to her husband, children, and above all her Lord, Jesus Christ! My siblings and I have been truly blessed to be the children of Jack and Jean Bliffen!

My daughter wrote the following poem after wearing my Mom's shoes to Easter service at Coal Run Church of Christ in 2021:

Grandma's Footprints
By Sarah Moon

Grandma wasn't at church this Easter, but her legacy was, still.
Grandma's shoes, they led us there; The family she built.
Sunday Morning; Easter lilies; Jesus is Alive!
Grandma taught us all to pray, Hosanna, in the Highest!
Grandma and Grandpa used to skate. They'd roll and stroll and dream.
I wonder if they dreamt of how far, the love they shared would reach.
"The stone was rolled away," they taught. We listened and believed.
Grandma and Grandpa's "Legacy of Faith"—A blessed legacy, indeed.
Grandma—We all miss her so, her song, her laugh, her grace—
So many things we love and miss on this side of eternity.
Grandma went to Heaven; We imagine the beauty she beholds.
She sings and skates, worships and prays, along the crystal shore.
Easter Sunday—ruffles and lace; Pretty dresses, coats, and ties;
Grandma's shoes still lead us there; a guiding footprint from the skies.
Grandpa loves his sweetheart so; He puts on his Easter coat and tie.
Grandma's home and she patiently waits; the end of his ministry
    is drawing nigh.
Grandma's footprints go beside him; Her faithful footsteps we still see.
Her support and submission evident; A Proverbs 31 woman,
    we all have seen.
"How beautiful are the feet of those who bring good news."
 Grandma's footprints continue to show us the
    Good News of Eternal Peace.

Jack Bliffen family
Row 1 - Grandchildren –
Morgan, Mary, Melissa, Marshall, Sarah, Bethany, Martin
Row 2 – Becky, John, Jane, Bob, Jean, Jack, Sheila, Jerry, Joni, Jim

Jack Bliffen family
Becky, John, Joni, Jim, Jean, Jack, Sheila, Jerry, Jane, Ed

Thomas family
Row 1 – Betty, Tom, Sheldon
Row 2 – Jonathan, Tim, David

Chapter 4

BETTY LOU AND SHELDON THOMAS

BY TOM THOMAS & JERRY BLIFFEN

Betty Lou, the third of nine children, was born to Ralph and Aleta Bliffen March 13, 1931. She grew up in Huntington and became a faithful member of the Sixth Avenue Church of Christ at a young age. She was always an attractive girl and many young men would attend church at Sixth Avenue to be near her. At one time, there were twelve boys in the youth choir who were interested in either Marie or Betty Bliffen. Of those twelve, ten of them went to Kentucky Christian College and most went into the ministry. When Betty's older brother Jack was at college, he would sometimes bring friends home with him on weekends. When she was a Senior in high school, Betty told Jack, "Bring me home a preacher." So, Jack did just that! He brought Sheldon Thomas home to meet Betty. Sheldon was from Lake Butler, Florida and had been influenced by his preacher to go to Kentucky Christian College. They were immediately interested in one another and began dating in the fall of 1949 when she enrolled at KCC.

Betty and Sheldon were married on July 21,1951 at the Sixth Avenue Church of Christ and served together in located ministries for the next 50 years. While Sheldon was a student at Kentucky Christian College, he had a weekend ministry in Farmers, Kentucky, near Morehead. His first full-time ministry was at the Westwood Christian Church in Ashland, Kentucky. He served there from 1951-1954. While ministering there, Betty and Sheldon were blessed with the births of their first two sons. Tim was born in Huntington on May 1, 1952, and Dave was born in Ashland on December 3, 1953.

In 1954 the Thomas family moved north to Martins Ferry, Ohio to serve the First Christian Church near the Ohio River. While serving there, they were blessed with the births of two more sons. Jonathan was born April 1, 1955 and Tom came along on March 20, 1958. Betty and Sheldon also experienced the loss of a stillborn daughter, though they seldom mentioned their grief.

Sheldon became the founding minister of the Westshore Christian Church (now New Beginnings Christian Church) in Tampa, Florida in 1959. They served there for eight years while the church grew and built their own building. Betty's parents, Ralph and Aleta, moved to Tampa as well in 1963, and became active members of the Westshore Church. In fact, after the Thomas family moved to a new ministry, her mother, Aleta became the Church Secretary.

One funny story that happened while the Thomas family was living in Tampa was the monkey story. It seems Uncle Joe decided to buy a monkey in Huntington and take it to Florida to give to the Thomas boys. He had a difficult and memorable time driving it to Florida because it was mean and would jump on him and try to bite him. I would say that caused a lot of distracted driving! After living with the Thomas family for a while, someone left the cage open and the monkey climbed up a telephone pole and started across a wire. It was doing okay until its tail touched another wire and it was immediately electrocuted and killed. Rumor has it that Betty left the cage open!

In 1967 the Thomas family moved north again to Fairfield, Illinois, where they served the First Christian Church until 1970. Tim and Dave, who were now in high school, developed some great friendships in Fairfield. Betty opened her home to their many friends and soon the youth group took off and grew tremendously. "The Fairfield Five", one of whom was

Tim, enrolled at Kentucky Christian College. The church continued to grow under Sheldon and Betty's leadership. Betty also served as a Volunteer at the hospital and was a Teacher's Aide in an elementary school.

In 1970 the family packed up and moved west to Dodge City, Kansas where Sheldon served as Minister of the First Christian Church at the top of Boot Hill. It was here that David and Jonathan were employed as characters in a live show reenactment of a gunfight. The boys would shoot each other and even fall off buildings in a show that would attract hundreds of visitors. While Sheldon was at Dodge City, he invited his brother-in-law, Jack, to preach a revival. At that time, Jack and Betty's youngest brother, Joe, was the Youth Minister there. It was a wonderful week of fellowship and revival as these three siblings served together in Dodge City. Sheldon had a fruitful ministry there and the church grew, but he was soon called to return to First Christian Church in Martins Ferry, Ohio in 1973.

Again, with great success in the ministry, Sheldon served at Martins Ferry for nine years. The church grew to over 600 in attendance! Sheldon's brother, Jake, came to help develop a Christian School, as he had previously been a school principal and administrator. Betty became the school's first director as well as the church's secretary. In the fall of 1976 twenty-one young people from that church became students at Kentucky Christian College, including Sheldon and Betty's youngest son, Tom! The Thomas family made so many good friends in Martins Ferry that Betty later returned to live there after Sheldon's death in Florida.

In 1982, the Thomas family was called back to Florida, this time to serve the First Christian Church in Pompano Beach on the east coast. This would become their longest ministry, as they served there for fifteen years. This became a bitter/sweet ministry for Betty and Sheldon. In 1988 their oldest son, Tim, was killed in an automobile accident, and five years later in 1993 their third son, Jonathan, was killed in a motorcycle accident. Tim was returning home from church on a Wednesday night, and Jonathan had just left an elderly lady's house after working on a project for her when he had his accident. Both became organ donors helping others to live on. Sheldon and Betty never really recovered from these tragedies. While at Pompano Beach,

Betty served as the church secretary and also became a dental assistant. The church experienced some growth in attendance during their time there.

In 1997-98 Sheldon and Betty served the Loxahatchee Christian Church, near West Palm Beach and then finished his ministry in a home church in Okeechobee from 1998-2001. Sheldon suffered with kidney problems his entire adult life. At one time he had over 100 kidney stones surgically removed from a kidney. The medication prescribed for his kidney disease attacked his liver and hastened his death. He received his eternal reward on March 26, 2001 at the age of 71.

Throughout his ministry, Betty was Sheldon's greatest helper. She taught Sunday School, led youth groups, served as church secretary, hosted home Bible study groups and even directed a Christian School. She took meals to shut-ins, gave people rides to the doctor or the store, babysat, and served in countless other ways. Betty loved people and it showed. She and Sheldon made others feel important and loved. They were a wonderful team of talent and dedication to the Lord and at the same time were humble and approachable to all.

Betty suffered with dementia the last 10 years of her life. During those years, her youngest son Tom and his wonderful wife, Lisa, cared for Betty's needs until she went home to be with her Lord, December 14, 2020 at the age of 89. She is interned beside her husband and two sons at the Swift Creek Cemetery in Lake Butler, Florida.

All four of the Thomas boys went to Bible College and served in the ministry. Tom and Dave have been full-time ministers and have led many people to Christ. Tim and Jonathan's lives were cut short, but they left a wonderful legacy of love and faith. Sheldon, Betty, Tim and Jonathan have left us for a better home, but their influence on thousands will live on for many years to come!

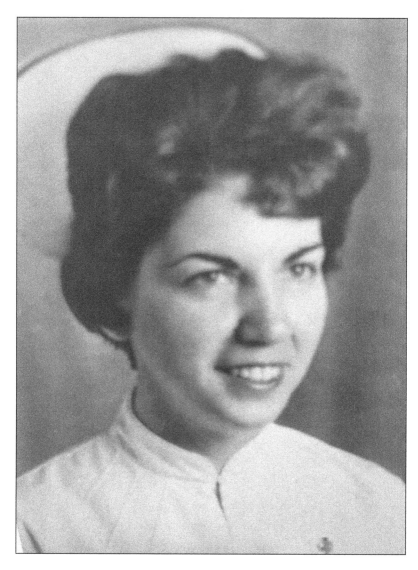

Mary

Chapter 5

MARY ELIZABETH BLIFFEN
BY JACK AND JERRY BLIFFEN

Mary Elizabeth Bliffen was born January 14, 1933 to Ralph and Aleta Bliffen in Huntington, West Virginia, the fourth of nine children. Mary had a very normal childhood, becoming a Christian at a young age. She lived a life of dedication to the Christian Church, primarily as a missionary nurse.

Mary was educated at Kentucky Christian College like all eight of her siblings. Her three sisters married preachers and four of her five brothers were preachers. She once commented, "I could have married any preacher I pleased, I just didn't please any of them!" She had a great sense of humor.

After graduation from college, at the suggestion of Dr. Denny Pruett, co-founder of Central Africa Christian Mission, Mary studied nursing at Kings Daughters Hospital in Ashland, Kentucky, where she specialized in Anesthesiology. She also studied Midwifery at the Frontier Graduate School of Midwifery in Hyden, Kentucky, not far from Hazard. The nursing school in Hyden was under the leadership of two British nurses from the Episcopal Church. At that time there were two churches in the area the nurses could attend. One was an Episcopal church in a community outside of Hyden called "Hell for Certain". The creek has the same name to this day. There was also a Church of Christ in Hyden. On Sundays, Mary would ask her nursing friends if they wanted to go to the Church of Christ or go to "Hell for Certain?" Later in life she became a Nurse Practitioner.

As a young woman Mary was not much of a cook. One time her older sister Marie wanted to attend a weekend Ladies Retreat, and Marie's husband John agreed, only if Mary would come to look after their girls and cook their meals. The only meal Sallie Jo can remember was hot dogs. Who can mess up hot dogs? Aunt Mary! Rather than boil them she said they would taste better broiled. The problem was she forgot about them until she smelled them burning! She was so worried about what John would say as she pealed the burnt skin off. But John didn't say a word.

Central Africa Christian Mission in Rhodesia, Africa was founded by John Pemberton and Dennis Pruett, two military veterans of World War II. Both of them were bemedaled heroes who barely escaped death and decided to serve the Lord at the end of the war. Dennis went to Winston Salem, North Carolina, to study medicine. He became a skilled surgeon and later specialized in brain surgery and hand surgery. He recruited several other surgeons to serve with him in Central Africa Christian Mission. The mission was founded to take over the work of some Church of Christ missionaries from New Zealand. One of them became the Prime Minister of Rhodesia. The Mission started many schools and churches, and after several years, John was even asked to become the Minister of Education for the country, which he declined.

Dennis and John recruited Mary to come as a missionary/nurse with Central Africa Christian Mission. At first, she was a Nurse Anesthetist in a hospital tent under a Baobab tree where the mission would later build a hospital. Her first case was sewing up 32 lacerations from a crocodile bite on a child! After she had delivered 42 babies, it was decided she should go to school to specialize in that field. She would later say that her greatest love was the children born in Africa with AIDS. She named the first baby she delivered in Africa "James" in honor of James Lowell Lusby, President of Kentucky Christian College. For 15 years, through the 60's and early 70's, Mary worked with the mission in Rhodesia.

During her time there, the mission built a house on the hospital grounds for nurses, where Mary lived when not working. The mission had the friendship of local farm families, who helped with their food supplies, including a lot of good beef from the cattle farms nearby! However, being in Mashoko, they were about 100 miles from Fort Victoria, the nearest city, now Masvingo. Monthly trips to the city in trucks kept the mission supplied with medicine and other necessary supplies. Because they had to ford three rivers on the trip, they were unable to make it in the six-month rainy season. Life there was never easy! Usually, one week a year, Mary would travel about 500 miles north to another mission in Chidamoyo to rest and visit with fellow missionaries, Ziden and Helen Nutt, Founders of Good News Productions International. According to Ziden, Mary would say, "After a year of nursing at Mashoko, I just need a week at the 'Nutt House.'" She would even do some nursing during her time there!

One time she was home on furlough and preparing the drinks at Marie's house for guests that would soon arrive. She said, "Isn't it interesting that here in the civilized United States we use our hands to put ice in the glasses. But in Africa we use ice tongs!" That was Mary!

Mary's work during her time in Rhodesia was primarily nursing, but she also taught some ladies' Bible classes. On one furlough, she asked her mother to join her in Africa as a house mother for the Bible College they had started in Salisbury, the capital city, now named Harare. Mary's Mother, Aleta, now widowed, went to Africa and worked for three years, moving to Mashoko to be in charge of the cleaning and laundry at the hospital for one year. Before Mary came home for the last time, she was working 16 hours a day, 7 days a week.

Mary's full financial support for her missionary work came from the ladies' group of the South Louisville Christian Church. They were faithful in this support for the entire term of her service to Central Africa Christian Mission. Her decision to leave was made when African nationals took over the government in an armed rebellion with intensions to kill every white person in the country. The nationals renamed the country Zimbabwe. Mary was also suffering with bouts of malaria, so her work for Christ in Africa ended. But her work for the Lord did not end there.

When Mary came home, she was physically and emotionally exhausted. She spent two years in Fort Pierce, Florida with her sister Peggy and husband Frank Bauer, who was the minister of the Southside Christian Church. After some time for recuperating, she went to work in the maternity wing of the hospital in Fort Pierce. She found it hard to understand how the other nurses could just work eight hours a day and then go home. After two months there, she was made the head nurse for her shift because she simply took control! Again, that was Mary!

After her two years in Florida, Mary went to be the nurse at Cookson Hills Children's' Home in Kansas, Oklahoma. She worked there ten years, during which time she provided a home and care for her Mother who was in failing health. Her Mother, Aleta, died in Mary's home. Mary had to leave Cookson Hills when she hurt her back and said, "I can't nurse children I can't pick up." While there, she also became the farm's butcher since she was very familiar with anatomy! Mary was now nearing retirement age, and she realized she had very little money, and had paid in very little to Social Security. She knew she needed to get a job that would allow her to draw more money through her retirement years. She found a great opportunity in the Bluegrass State.

Kentucky had built a State Penitentiary in West Liberty in 1990 for 2000 inmates. At that time, Mary's younger brother, Steve, was the minister of the West Liberty Christian Church and had started a prison ministry at the penitentiary. Mary moved to West Liberty and was hired as a medical professional for the prison. The inmates called her "The Queen of Mean" since they thought she enjoyed giving painful shots. However, they were glad to see her most of the time, because she dispensed their medicine! Steve conducted weekly church services at the prison every Sunday evening, and Mary was often the song leader. The inmates grew to love their preacher and song leader/nurse. Before he died in 1999, Steve had baptized over 180 prisoners! Mary thoroughly enjoyed working with her brother in this prison ministry.

During some of the time that Mary lived in West Liberty, she lived in a farmhouse owned by Aunt Lynn Bliffen's brother, Chuck Woodhouse. Sallie Jo's husband, Phillip Nickell, loved to kid with Mary and once told her to be careful because all the women in the area were getting pregnant from the water. She replied that she didn't have a thing to worry about because she bought bottled water to drink. Then Phillip said, "Yes, but you bathe in it, don't you?" They all had a big laugh!

One Saturday evening in 2002, Mary was tending to her niece, Rose Anne, who had broken her arm. Mary said, "If I didn't know better, I would say I was having a heart attack." The next morning, she didn't show up for church. Her nephew and preacher who was hired after Steve's death, Tom Thomas, found her dead in her bed that afternoon at the age of 69. Mary had spent her life taking care of other people, and some of us had wondered, who would take care of Mary in her later years? That question was answered that Lord's day in December. The One who had cared for her all her life had taken her home! Her body is buried beside her parents in Huntington.

Affectionately called "Uncle Mary," by her nieces and nephews, she was always the favorite person at any family gathering. It was understood by all that "where Uncle Mary is, that's where the party is!" She was always ready for a good card game; her laugh was contagious and would make the entire family smile with delight! She had a beautiful voice which she used for the Lord, singing many solo's in church and leading singing when needed. In commenting on her life, she said, "It is a good thing I never married. If I had, I could not have done my mission work. I would have had to be with my husband." When she was going to Africa the last time, another missionary nurse had just been killed in a neighboring country. Pondering this event, Mary said, "If I am killed over there, don't spend money to have my body returned to America, use that money to send another missionary." Then she got on the airplane. On December 1, 2002, Mary took her final flight! That was Mary!

Bauer family
Robin, Frank, Tracy, Peggy, Terrie

Chapter 6

PEGGY ANN AND FRANK BAUER
BY TERRIE HOLDEN AND JERRY BLIFFEN

Peggy Ann Bliffen, the fifth of nine children of Ralph and Aleta, was born September 2, 1934 in Huntington. She, like her siblings, became a member of the Sixth Avenue Church of Christ at a young age. Peggy's nickname growing up was "Olive Oil" because she was so thin. She wore her sisters' hand me downs until she was married. After graduating from Huntington East High School, she enrolled at Kentucky Christian College in 1954. She soon met Frank Bauer who was studying for the ministry. One time my Dad, Jack, took Frank home to Huntington for a weekend and there was a warm chocolate cake on the table. Frank really wanted a piece of it, but Dad said to wait until it cooled and they went into the living room. Soon they heard the backdoor open and close and heard "HAHA!" The door opened again and they heard "HOHO!" Then the door opened a third time and they heard "HEHE!" Jack yelled to Frank, "Run!" They ran to the kitchen and found the younger brothers had divided the cake into thirds and it was gone! Frank said he learned to run on the "HAHA!"

Frank and Peggy were married in Huntington on April 8, 1956, during their Sophomore year. Peggy wore her sister Marie's wedding dress after her Mother altered it to fit. For the next two years Frank and Peggy lived on campus of Kentucky Christian College in the last of a line of log cabins. Their cabin was near the college barn where mice were plentiful. Because the cold winter wind would blow through the cabin walls, Peggy tacked a quilt to the wall to block the cold draft. However, mice set up housekeeping between the wall and the quilt so she had to take it down. Both Frank and Peg graduated from Kentucky Christian College in 1958.

Frank's first ministry was at the Peeled Oak Christian Church near Owingsville, Kentucky. He served there from 1956-59. Their first child was born while living there. Their first two children were daughters, Terrie and Robin. Their only son, Tracy, was born in 1960. Sadly, Tracy passed away in 2012 at age 52. In 1959 the Bauer family moved 40 miles east to Olive Hill, where they enjoyed a successful ministry for seven years at First Christian Church, not far from Grayson where my family lived. We enjoyed many visits with the Bauers during those years. I still remember Uncle Frank making delicious chocolate fudge, pouring it out on the counter, letting it cool, then cutting it to share with all of us! Terrie recalled one funny story from Olive Hill. It was shortly after President Kennedy was assassinated. Her Mother, Peggy, was leading the singing in Sunday school and a Pentecostal Holiness lady was visiting that particular morning. When the visitor suddenly put her hands in the air, Peggy fell to the floor! She thought that lady had a gun!

In 1966 the Bauers moved to Ohio where Frank became the minister of the East Dayton Christian Church. Then in 1970 they moved to Atlanta, Georgia where Frank ministered to the Central Christian Church. This church was near Atlanta Christian College where my Dad was Vice President. One time our family and the Bauers went to Six Flags Over Georgia amusement park and it rained. Most visitors left the park, but not us! We rode the roller coasters over and over till we lost count. It was all we teenagers could do to keep up with Uncle Frank! He was always so much fun!

In 1971 the Bauers moved further south to Leesburg, Florida where Frank ministered to the First Christian Church for three years. Next, they moved even further south to Fort Pierce to serve the Southside Christian Church from 1974-1982. While ministering in Fort Pierce, Frank was trimming palm fonds in the church yard when one of them fell on a power line. Electricity went through the branch into the ladder. Frank fell off the ladder being held by Peggy and landed feet first on the sidewalk below. He broke his leg and ankle but still preached the next Sunday from a wheelchair. The people called him "Preacher Ironsides."

In 1982 Frank and Peggy moved back to Kentucky to serve the First Christian Church in Monticello in the southern part of the Bluegrass State. Then around 1986 they were called back to the church in East Dayton, Ohio. After serving there for around six years, they moved back to Florida to minister to the First Christian Church in Arcadia. After about five years, Frank and Peggy started the New Hope Christian Church in Arcadia in 1997, where they served until his death in 2010. In fact, he preached twice thirteen days before he passed away and taught a Bible study ten days before going to his heavenly home.

Frank was always well dressed and his shoes were shined! Peggy always looked nice and both had smiling faces! After Frank and Peggy married, she never worked outside the church. Peg was always Frank's secretary, sometimes paid and sometimes volunteer. After Frank's death, his daughters saw to Peggy's needs. Peggy passed away at age 87 on December 8, 2021 in New Lisbon, Indiana and was buried beside her husband in Arcadia, Florida. She and Frank served together in 54 years of ministry as faithful servants of our Lord. They served nine Christian Churches in four different states! What a wonderful legacy of faith!

Jerry H. and family
Row 1-Ricky, Micky
Row 2-Aleta, Jerry, Judy, Mary

Chapter 7

JERRY HARRISON AND
JUDY BLIFFEN
BY JUDY AND JERRY *DAVID* BLIFFEN

Jerry Harrison Bliffen was born April 11, 1937, the sixth of nine children born to Ralph and Aleta. He was baptized into Christ at nine years of age at Sixth Avenue Church of Christ in Huntington, West Virginia. As a youngster, Jerry was given the nickname "Jiggs" from a comic strip, "Jiggs & Maggie." Jerry was "Jiggs," and his sister Mary was "Maggie." Mary's nickname didn't stick, but "Jiggs" did!

As a teen, his first job was delivering newspapers. After graduating from high school, Jerry followed his siblings' tradition of enrolling at Kentucky Christian College. While a student there, he was a starter on the basketball team and a bass singer in the concert choir.

Jerry met his future wife, Judy Moon, his sophomore year of college. Judy was raised in Smithers, West Virginia, just southeast of Charleston, and came to Kentucky Christian College for a Bible education. Before going to college, Judy's family had moved to Huntington and became members of the Highlawn Church of Christ, where Paul Bennett was the minister. Paul died in an airplane crash on Pine Mountain near Grundy, Virginia in 1965. Jerry and Judy were married on July 7, 1958 and lived in a log cabin at KCC while finishing their college years.

Denny Pruett recruited Jerry to go to Africa as a missionary to help with Central Africa Christian Mission. He was to work in the lab at Mishoko Hospital, so to prepare for that, Jerry attended a lab training school in Saint Louis, Missouri. During this time, he also traveled, trying to raise support for his future mission work. This proved to be difficult and he was unsuccessful in raising enough support for his family to go to the mission field. While Jerry was at Saint Louis, Judy went back to Milton, West Virginia where her parents lived. It was here that she gave birth to their first daughter, Mary, on March 7, 1959.

After the door closed for mission work in Africa, Jerry's first located ministry was at Knifley, Kentucky, close to Liberty, where his sister, Marie and her husband John Stumbo were ministering at that time. Jerry and Judy enjoyed visiting with them on occasion. While in Kentucky, Jerry and Judy had their second daughter, Aleta on March 23, 1960. The ministry at Knifley lasted a couple of years before the family moved to Milton, West Virginia. Jerry worked at a few different jobs in that area before his employment with the Greyhound Bus Lines. He loved driving for Greyhound, and he continued in this profession for 25 years (1964-1989). Judy gave birth to their third child, Ricky on January 7, 1962, while living in Milton.

Jerry requested a transfer to Florida because he did not like driving the bus in the snow. They moved to Tampa and stayed there one year. It was during that year that their second son, Micky came along on March 22, 1965. They enjoyed being close to Jerry's parents, but Judy did not like Tampa and was homesick for the Mountain State. She indicated that she still misses her West Virginia home to this day. So, after a year in Tampa, they moved back to West Virginia. Because Jerry's job with Greyhound, the family moved a few times in West Virginia. In every move, Jerry found a church where he could serve the Lord, especially teaching God's Word. In 1967, Uncle "Jiggs" had a regular run every other day from West Virginia to Ohio that crossed the Silver Bridge at Point Pleasant. He crossed the Silver Bridge with about 40 people on his bus on December 15, 1967 just one hour before it collapsed into the Ohio River. Forty-six people plunged to their death on that dreadful day, two of whom were never found. God was watching over

Uncle "Jiggs" and his passengers on that cold December afternoon, just ten days before Christmas.

In 1974, Jerry and Judy moved to Jacksonville, Florida to again get away from the snowy driving in the Mountain State. It was in the city of Orange Park on the southwest side of Jacksonville, that they settled. Because there was no Christian Church in Orange Park, the Bliffens and others from the Mandarin Christian Church in Jacksonville started the Orange Park Christian Church in 1978. Jerry served this new congregation as one of the charter elders. During his years of driving for Greyhound from Jacksonville to Fort Lauderdale he would memorize the books of the Bible in different ways, in fact, 91 different ways; forwards, backwards, alphabetically, skipping every other book, outside in, inside out, etc. One time he missed his turn off to Fort Lauderdale because of his deep focusing on the Bible books!

In 1989, Greyhound drivers and other employees went on strike. Jerry did not want to cross the picket lines, so his Greyhound career ended at that time. Soon after, Jerry and Judy moved to Dothan, Alabama, where Jerry served as Minister of a new struggling congregation. He served there for a couple of years until the church found itself without enough funds to continue. The church dissolved and Jerry and Judy attended a nearby non-instrumental Church of Christ. During the Dothan years, both Jerry and Judy volunteered with a Hospice program in their community. After a time, Jerry was hired to be the Hospice Chaplain. They lived in Dothan throughout the 90's before moving back to Orange Park where Jerry, Judy and their daughter Mary all worked in a storage business.

Jerry and Judy had heartbreaking days and years, losing both of their sons, Ricky and Micky, to heart attacks. Ricky died at the age of 49 in 2011, and Micky died at the age of 52 in 2018. Their oldest daughter, Mary, still lives in Jacksonville as do her twins, Matt and Andy. She also has a son, Jeffrey, who lives in Japan. Mary lost her oldest son, Jeremy, in a car accident in Alabama in 1996.

Daughter Aleta (named for our Grandmother, Aleta Bliffen) met her husband, Don Hulsey, at Johnson Bible College. They dedicated twenty-one years of their lives to mission work in Mozambique, Africa. Though Jerry and Judy were never able to go to Africa as missionaries, their daughter and her husband did! Don currently ministers to the Port Caroline Christian Church in Jacksonville. They have three children.

Jerry grew a beard that turned white. The last time I saw him he looked a lot like Santa Claus and had the compassionate spirit of that jolly old soul as well! For many years Judy has cared for her sister, Kitty, who has Downs Syndrome. Kitty now also has dementia, which makes her care even more challenging for Judy. But with God's help, she continues to see to Kitty's needs day after day.

One Sunday morning in 2016 Jerry had an upset stomach and was unable to attend church. At this time, he was serving as a facilitator for grief support group in Jacksonville. He attended a support group meeting the next day (Monday) and at the end of the session he turned in his files to another counselor. On Tuesday he began struggling to breathe and was transported to the hospital by ambulance. His doctor was optimistic about his recovery and said, "Jerry will be a new man by morning." And he was right! Jerry entered into Heaven on September 13, 2016 at 10:30 pm. After 79 years of living his life for the Lord, His work on earth was over, but Jerry Harrison's legacy of love, faith and compassion live on. I am proud to be named after my Uncle Jerry!

Steve and family
Row 1 - Lynn, Steve
Row 2 – Scott, Jeff, Amy, Chad

Chapter 8

STEPHEN DEAN AND
LYNN BLIFFEN
BY LYNN BLIFFEN THOMSEN,
JEFF AND JERRY BLIFFEN

Stephen Dean Bliffen was the seventh child born to Ralph and Aleta on March 27, 1941 in Huntington. Like his siblings, he became a member of the Sixth Avenue Church of Christ at a young age. After his high school graduation, he enrolled at Kentucky Christian College where he met his future wife, Lynn Woodhouse. Lynn was from Joliet, Illinois, and had attended two years at Lincoln Christian College, but after visiting Kentucky Christian College, she decided to transfer for her Junior year. She soon made many friends, including Steve! Lynn did not know at that time that Steve was engaged to a young lady from Olive Hill. But after a month, Steve broke his engagement and asked Lynn for a date. That was the beginning of a wonderful relationship that lasted until Steve's passing to heaven in 1999. In college, Lynn was a cheerleader and Steve was a basketball player, and both were very well liked and admired on campus. They were married on August 9, 1963. Their first full time ministry was from 1963-65 at Leakesville, North Carolina. While serving there Lynn gave birth to their first son, Scott in 1964.

In 1965, they moved to Cedar Lake, Indiana, where Steve served as minister and Camp Manager for Lake Region Christian Assembly. While in Indiana, a second son was born in 1966, Jeff. Both Scott and Jeff would later become elders in Christian churches in the Bluegrass State.

Steve's longest and most productive ministry was in West Liberty, Kentucky! The family moved there in 1969 where Steve served as the minister of the West Liberty Christian Church for 30 years. Amy was born in 1969 and Chad completed their family of six in 1975. At this time Steve was described by Jeff as "a 6-foot 4-inch, 240-pound man with black hair, olive skin, kind eyes, and a warrior's spirit!" He was declared by the Licking Valley Courier Newspaper as "the Conscience of Morgan County". He was a polarizing figure. Some loved him and some hated him, but all respected him. Steve was a faithful and fearless follower of Jesus Christ, which at times caused him to be a disrupter of the status quo. He fought against alcohol sales, illegal drugs, and the sale of pornography. He also fought for judicial integrity. Some of these stands led to some nasty consequences --- threatening phone calls all hours of the day and night, being cursed out on Main Street, threatened with a gun, being spit at, mutilated animals thrown into his yard, dynamite placed on his back porch, shotgun blasts breaking out windows and doors on the parsonage, attempts to run him off the road, and burning his car! Through it all Steve remained calm and resolute. His motto was "do the right thing." He never returned evil for evil, but he never backed down either. He always said, "I have a lot of people behind me --- way behind me!" Then he would laugh; he had a great sense of humor.

Steve was a lover of sports. He was good at golf and tennis but didn't have much time to play. In basketball he could consistently hit a long hook shot and loved playing Industrial/Church League softball. Jeff remembers him most as an outstanding volleyball player. Steve was a natural court leader! His team would be behind by 10 or more points and he would bring his team back to victory. He would huddle with his team and say, "we just need to win this next point." He would continue to say this with every point until his team won! He loved board games and cards! He would always laugh when he ripped the heart out of his opponents. Like all Bliffens, he did not like to lose! We got that from Grandma Bliffen. Steve had a garden every year and when the tomatoes came in, he would eat a BLT every day for lunch. The family also canned vegetables from the garden.

During his located ministry Steve took short term mission trips to Haiti, Mexico, the Dominican Republic, and even smuggled Bibles into Russia! He visited the Holy Land several times. He and his church supported Mary and Grandma Bliffen in their mission work in Rhodesia, Africa. They also provided a place for Mary to live when she was home from Africa. Steve served as dean for several weeks of camp at Howell's Mill Christian Assembly. He was President of the local Ministerial Association for years. The police would send any drifter or indigent to him. The family would never know who might be at the door when someone came knocking. They would sometimes take in foster children or runaways for short periods of time.

One of Steve's sermons had a big impact on Lynn. The title was, "Give of Your Best to the Lord." A few days later a little homeless man came to the door. It was winter and he said he was cold. Lynn went looking for a coat for him and found 2 of Steve's coats. One was thread bare and the other was a brand-new trench coat Steve had received at Christmas. Lynn thought of Steve's sermon, "Give of Your Best to the Lord." Later that day Steve said, "Lynn, have you seen my new trench coat?" Lynn confessed what she had done and said, "You should have seen him in your new coat. It looked like a full-length dress with the sleeves rolled up! I'm sure he will stay warm." They laughed about that for years.

Steve was a good preacher and excellent counselor! He led many souls to Christ and helped to save many marriages! His secret to counseling was his ability to listen. Once he listened to someone for three hours. He said, "Most people have the ability to solve their own problems, they just need to talk long enough to arrive at that point and be heard by another person who will hold their confidence."

As a community leader, Steve was second to none! He was Lieutenant Governor of the Kiwanis Club which provided community fireworks and games on the 4th of July. They developed and ran a community pool, parks and playgrounds, tennis courts, baseball fields, and more. He loved working at the Kiwanis Club bean pot during the annual Sorghum Festival every September. He also served on the Board of Christian Homes of Kentucky and as Morgan County Football Chaplain. Ironically, Steve became Chairman of the Board at his alma mater, Kentucky Christian College, where he had been kicked off campus for water fights when he was a student. When Sheila and I graduated from Kentucky Christian College in 1976, Uncle Steve gave us 5 Bicentennial $2 bills that we have to this day. He was a big help in the college reaching University status and developing the Wayne B. Smith Building for ministerial studies. This is funny because Wayne always said, "I steal most of my sermons from Bob Russell!" Brother Wayne preached many times at West Liberty and he and Steve became good friends.

Steve was supposed to graduate from Kentucky Christian College in 1963 but it was delayed until 1971 because he "neglected" to turn in a paper for Tom Gemeinhart's class! On his Graduation Day in 1971, he "neglected" to attend because he was on the golf course with Uncle Joe and Dick Damron. They took off their hats for a moment of silence on the 9th hole in honor of graduation, then finished their game and went out to eat!

The first Volunteer Chaplain at the Eastern Kentucky Correctional Complex at West Liberty was Steve Bliffen. He would go up to the "Big House," as Mary called it, every Sunday evening and conduct a worship service. I had the privilege of speaking there on a few occasions. Aunt Mary, who worked there as a nurse, would sing and Steve would preach. He baptized close to 200 inmates into Christ! He really had two churches he served in West Liberty.

Steve was diagnosed with colon cancer in 1995. He managed it like everything else in life --- with prayer, humor, and determination. After he had a colostomy, I met him at Paintsville to play golf. About halfway through our round he went down into a brook and cleaned out his colostomy bag and kept on playing! We had a great time! Steve had 13 surgeries in four years, but handled it all with grace, dignity, a smile, and a lot of God! He would push his IV pole down the hall and visit and pray with other patients. The nurses loved him very much. They even made him a diploma on his marker board that said, "To the bravest patient we have ever had!" He kept on preaching, even from his recliner, until two months before his death on February 25th, 1999. His son, Jeff said of his Dad, "He preached a lot of sermons, but the best was the way he lived and his confidence as he died. I hope to live well and die well as he did!" His loving wife, Lynn said, "He always had a wonderful sense of humor. I think besides prayer, this got him through a lot. He was my hero and I miss him to this day!"

Steve's funeral service overflowed the West Liberty Christian Church building! At his death he was one of the most loved and respected men in Morgan County. His body is buried in a West Liberty cemetery less than 200 yards from the church. We are all looking forward to our family reunion in Heaven at the feet of Jesus!

I Know A Man
By Scott Bliffen

I know a man that is honest, humble and honorable
This man is above reproach, respected and revered.
He has always preached love, loyalty and everlasting life
He lives his life fruitfully, faithfully and fearlessly.
He makes a stand for what he believes in, for who he befriends
    and for benevolence.
He is always positive, perceptive and peaceful.
I know a man that is accountable, able and admired.
He does good things, gives great advice, and gives of himself.
He is a counselor, a comforter and is compassionate
He has standards, he is selfless and has self-control.
He unites people, understands people and uplifts people.
He is bold, believed and beloved.
He is caring, clever and courteous.
He is kind, knowledgeable and is a keeper of the faith.
He is helpful, humorous and happy.
He works hard, is very wise and doesn't worry about
    what people think of him.
He has stood up to temptation and has been through
    trials and tribulations.
He is an encourager, an evangelist and an example to everyone.

I know a man that is everything I want to be.
If you think that the man that I know is my Dad, good, but it is not.
The man I know is Jesus Christ.
We can't physically see Christ except through the Bible
    and through peoples' lives.
In 1 Corinthians 11:1 Paul says, "Follow my example as I follow
    the example of Christ."
I believe with all honesty and sincerity that my Dad can say the exact
    words that Paul said, "Follow my example as
    I follow the example of Christ."
He fights the good fight and finishes the race.
So, I know a man that is like the man that I want to be like.

John H. and family
Diane, John, Sandy, Sheri

Chapter 9

John Hamilton and Sandy Bliffen
By Jerry and John H. Bliffen

John Hamilton Bliffen was born October 24, 1942 in Huntington to Ralph and Aleta Bliffen, the eighth of nine children. John graduated from Huntington East High School in 1960. At the young age of 8 his brother Jack was preaching a revival at the Sixth Avenue Church of Christ when both John and his younger brother Joe were baptized into Christ by their oldest brother. John attended church camp every year from the 6th through the 12th grade, first at KCC, then at Howells Mill Christian Assembly.

John attended 2 years at Kentucky Christian College (1960-62) in Grayson, where he played basketball and won a lot of games. He was awarded the Sportsmanship Trophy both years! He also went to the local jail most Sunday's where he led a short devotion with the inmates. At KCC he also met his wife, Sandra Sue Myers of Williamson, West Virginia. She was the daughter of Wallace and Wilba Lee (Romans) Myers. They married on September 12, 1962. The ceremony was performed by his brother, Jack Bliffen, at the Fifth Avenue Church of Christ in Williamson. Sandra suffered with several medical problems through her life and died on October 2, 2020, after 58 years of faithful marriage!

Following their wedding they moved to Tampa, Florida where they lived for 5 years. John worked at the Tampa Tribune-Times newspaper as an apprentice printer, following in his father's profession. While in Tampa John was active with the Westshore Christian Church serving as a Deacon and Sunday School teacher.

They moved to Huntington in 1967 where John worked at the Commercial Printing Company as a Linotype operator for three months. Then they moved to Dayton, OH where John worked at the Dayton Daily News for 38 years in various positions until retiring in 2007. John and Sandy became charter members of the Valley View Christian Church in Englewood, Ohio in 1968. They moved to Franklin in 1973 where they lived for 15 years before moving to Troy where John continues to live at this writing.

While in Franklin, John was very active in church work at the First Christian Church. Over the years he was a Sunday School Teacher, Sunday School Superintendent, Treasurer, Deacon and Elder.

John and Sandy were blessed with 2 daughters, Sheri and Diane. John baptized both girls in the late 70's. Sheri married Samuel K. Fox in 1994. They have 4 children, Caitlyn, Nicholas, and twins Rachael and Lindsey. Caitlyn has two daughters, Addison and Riley. Sheri is a registered nurse working in the NICU at Children's Hospital in Cincinnati.

Diane married Brian Paul West in 1985. They have 3 children, Zachary, Luke and Faith. Diane is a teacher in a Christian school in Akron, OH.

At 79 years of age, John has remained physically active, enjoying playing Pickleball about 5 days a week. He continues to enjoy good health and is a tremendous blessing to his family and church.

Joe and family
Row 1 – Joe, Nonta
Row 2 – Erin, Devon

Chapter 10

James Joseph (Joe) Bliffen
By Nonta Miller, John H. Bliffen, Erin Simpson and Jerry Bliffen

J oe was the last of 9 children born to Ralph and Aleta, but he was not the least! He outgrew all of his siblings to 6 feet 6 inches and was an outstanding basketball player. Joe was born in Huntington on October 18, 1943 and after graduating high school, enrolled at Kentucky Christian College in 1961, following the example of 4 brothers and 4 sisters. He turned down several scholarship opportunities to play basketball in college and decided to prepare for the ministry. Joe was a big fish in a little pond at KCC! He received many trophies and honors the 4 years he played for the Knights. His career included 1897 points, 1009 rebounds (a school record,) a single game record of 49 points on November 19, 1964, and a single game record of 28 rebounds. He averaged 25 points a game throughout his 4 years and his career Field Goal Percentage of 51.3% was another school record. When the Knights needed a basket in the early 1960's they would "get the ball to Joe!" As a boy, I really enjoyed watching him play and wanted to be like him. His number, 52, was officially retired in 2006 at a home game in Grayson. On that occasion Joe was photographed standing by his teammates John Bliffen and Leon Schrader, as well as his coach, Loren Dace, and coach and long-time friend, Dick Damron. On one occasion while I was a student at

KCC in the early 70's, Joe spoke at a chapel service and I still remember him saying he "had put away his trophies and now was using his books!"

Joe married Nonta Smith and they had 2 daughters, Erin and Devon Jo. His first full-time ministry was in Unionport, Ohio where he served from 1967-72. He then moved to Dodge City, Kansas, where he served as youth minister at the Christian Church on Boot Hill for a year, where his brother-in-law, Sheldon Thomas was the Senior Minister. In 1973 Joe and family moved back to Ohio to serve as senior minister for the La Belle View Church of Christ in Steubenville, where he ministered for 14 years. He had a very successful ministry at LaBelle View and served as camp dean for several Senior weeks of church camp. In 1987 Joe accepted the ministry of the Sunbury Christian Church, just north of Columbus. Here he enjoyed another successful ministry until 1998.

Throughout Joe's ministry he took several mission trips and led trips to the Holy Land. He and his brother Steve even smuggled Bibles into Russia! Sadly, Joe and Nonta divorced around 1998 and both remarried. Joe married Sara in May of 1999. He was out of the ministry for a while and did secular work until becoming the minister of the Fourth Avenue Christian Church (Disciples of Christ) in Columbus. His brother John said that Fourth Avenue was very liberal, but Joe never wavered from Biblical teachings. John even told Joe that he was "a missionary to the Disciples." Joe met the staff from the Disciples headquarters head on and let them know he was more qualified to minister and had more credentials than they possessed! Joe never lost sight of who he was and what he stood for. He remained true to his core beliefs until he died. He was still ministering at Fourth Avenue when he died of pancreatic cancer on July 2, 2014 at 70 years of age.

One story I remember about Joe happened one summer in the early 60's. He was working on campus for the college under my Dad's supervision. I was aggravating him, just as any mean little nephew would do. He got so mad at me that he tied me to a tree and left me there. I don't remember who finally untied me, but it wasn't Joe! He got in trouble, but we both learned a lesson from that experience. I never bothered him again and I still looked up to him in more ways than one! I, like my Heavenly Father, loved Joe and found grace and forgiveness in my heart for his shortcomings. He was a giant among men and greatly loved by those who really knew him!

My Dad
By Erin Bliffen Simpson

James Joseph BIiffen was born in Huntington on 18 October,1943 to Ralph and Aleta Bliffen. The youngest of nine children, I do not get the feeling that Dad was given any breaks for being the littlest, as when he misbehaved, Grandmother Aleta had no reservations in informing the youngest of the "three little boys" that Grandfather Ralph would promptly take care of business on his return from work. Dad never talked of poverty, but of love and care from his mother, and although Grandfather Ralph was often silent and seemed to keep much of his wisdom to himself, was a constant and steady presence in my dad's life. Dad talked about Grandfather Ralph's enjoyment of lifting weights, riding motorcycles, and I believe swimming. I'm happy to know that Ralph had a funny side, as evidenced by a photo I have with him wearing a wig and smiling into the camera. This is special to me.

I know that the Bliffens were not well off financially, but I guess that was probably the daily life of most families in those days in Huntington. Dad talks about holes in his shoes, sharing a bedroom with several brothers, and watching Aleta get creative in the kitchen, stretching food as far as she could. Dad talked often about Bliffen Burgers, Christmas date nut rolls, and early morning breakfasts of hot potatoes that also doubled as hand warmers on cold morning walks to school.

I know Aleta was proud of the Bliffen family when I look at the old Christmas cards. Grandmother Aleta sent around an annual Christmas card with all the family represented in the card, and it is fun to see the family additions year to year. For a long time, my dad had a Christmas ornament with Grandmother and Grandfather's picture, along with all the pictures of the nine kids. I remember taking the ornament in my hands, spinning it around, and trying to imagine all those dark headed kids together, playing cards, riding bikes, and sitting around Aleta's table on New Year's Eve, apparently the party of the year for all the kids in the neighborhood. I understand these parties went on until the early morning hours of New Year's Day, and Grandmother Aleta loved every minute of it. I remember seeing a newspaper article about these famous parties, and I wished I could travel back in time to be a part of one.

I don't know when Ralph and Aleta became Christians, but I know that their faith was of utmost importance to them, and my dad talked of sitting between his parents at church every Sunday, probably fidgeting and squirming as most boys will do. Many Sundays, Grandfather Ralph would quietly pass my Dad a $20.00 bill wrapped in a $1.00 bill, and Dad would dutifully place that $21.00 in the offering plate. This quiet and consistent habit taught my dad the value of tithing, and he was a steady example of tithing for his entire life. To my Dad, tithing was not only financial, but through his life took great pains to care for the churches that were entrusted to him. He spent countless hours working inside and out of these facilities. I remember all the building, mowing, painting, and caring he put into these churches. He knew the church was the body of Christ, and also knew that the building itself was a reflection of the people who inhabited it, and made sure that the buildings were tidy, inviting, and well loved. My Dad's love for the church was for me, an active and vibrant living offering to the people of Jesus.

As to the mundane, everyday kind of happenings, my Dad's office door was always open. I loved walking into his office at the LaBelle View Church of Christ in Steubenville Ohio. His office was filled with intimidating looking books, odd and exotic looking souvenirs from his travels to Russia, Poland and Mexico, and of course, pictures that Devon and I had drawn and painted over our childhood years. His office smelled of musty papers and old wood and felt important to me, holy almost, and I never felt intimidated, but I knew that a lot of prayer and meditating happened in that room. When we would visit him, he was always writing in his neat and even looping handwriting...sermons, letters, notes, etc. He was a massive yet gentle presence behind his desk, always dressed neatly in slacks and a buttoned shirt, but usually had a change of clothes in his leather satchel for playing basketball or going to swim at the Weirton YMCA.

My Dad loved sports. He was an avid and talented basketball player for Kentucky Christian College and in fact in his later years, his basketball number was retired, as he was so advanced in his basketball playing skills. Word had it that he could have had a full ride scholarship to a college in Florida where his parents had recently moved, but he was set about the business of the ministry. I'll also tell you that man could play softball. Boy how he could play! At Elkhorn Valley Christian Service Camp in Bergholz, Ohio Joe Bliffen's softball hits were legendary, and there were tales that he could hit the softball all the way to the white barn across the road and up the hill. I do not know if this tale is true, but I believe more than one camper would attest to that feat.

Dad was often the dean of summer camp for Elkhorn Valley, and I can attest to the fact that his week was, hands down, everyone's favorite Senior Week of the summer. All the kids respected and admired him, and when it was time for all the new love birds to say good night at the end of the day, Dad would ring that camp bell firmly and begin to make his way to the top of the hill where the dorms were situated. I can tell you right now every kid knew he'd better make himself scarce by the time my Dad made it to the top, because tomorrow night, that kid would be walking with my Dad from the bell to the dorm.

I have many pictures of myself in my Dad's arms at Elkhorn Valley Christian Service Camp as a baby, a small child, and then along the front row, squinting into the sun at the camera, knowing he and my Mom were somewhere behind me, smiling and holding hands. I loved those days at church camp! I was so proud that my Dad was the best dean of the whole summer. I remember he was the dean of camp the week that Elvis Presley died. We had heard the news via Pat Mack, the camp secretary who had heard it on the radio. The teenage girls at camp were beside themselves with angst and woe, crying the blues into each other's shoulders. My Dad told them to "get over it." I always loved him for that.

My Dad had four churches in the span of his life, that I know of, anyway. The first was Unionport Church of Christ in Unionport Ohio, which started around 1968. I was a small baby during that time, and Dad was the youth minister and eventually worked his way to ministering at that congregation. While he didn't stay long there, maybe four or five years, he made lifelong friends and even today, Unionport folks will tell me how much they loved Joe Bliffen. In about 1973, my parents moved 45 minutes from Unionport to Steubenville, and I believe this is truly where his life's ministry lay. He was the minister at the La Belle View Church of Christ for about 13 years, and during that time saw a lot of growth in the church. I remember the pews being packed, even on a regular Sunday morning. Forget about Christmas and Easter. Those days were standing room only. My Dad really honed his preaching skills here, and was a dynamic and thoughtful preacher, true to the Word of God and plain in his speech. "Where the Bible speaks, we speak; where the Bible is silent, we are silent." These words even today ring in my own mind as I read passages from his Bible, given to me after his passing. He was a true scholar of the Bible and loved the exegesis of scripture. It was truly his life's passion.

Dad and Mom had a brief stint as Youth Minister at a church in Dodge City Kansas at some point during this time, although I was too small and too many years have passed for me to know the particulars of this move. We moved there with Uncle Sheldon and Aunt Betty and stayed for just a year. Perhaps the church wasn't a good fit or maybe they all just longed for the Ohio Valley, but they returned to Steubenville and Martins Ferry, and I believe they picked up as though nothing had ever happened. It was around this time,1974, that my younger sister was born. Devon Jo was born on June 30, 1974, and she was a living doll. Dad adored her, and I remember him dozing on the sofa with her in his arms. I wish I had known as a 5-year-old how lovely this was, but we can never know things when we are children, can we?

After I graduated in 1987, my Dad, Mom and Devon moved to Sunbury Ohio, at which time I went on to Kentucky Christian College and Dad became the minister at the Sunbury Church of Christ. As in Steubenville, the folks at Sunbury loved my Dad, and they valued his preaching and teaching. My Mother, Nonta, started a very successful preschool at the church, and the two of them carried on traditions they had started at La Belle View...a weekly pitch in dinner on Wednesday nights, spectacular Fourth of July celebrations, cantatas, and original plays complete with full-on sets. My Dad even became the Choir Director, and he didn't do half bad!

In about 1993, after I had graduated college, my Dad got very sick from a small cut while helping build an addition onto the church. They had been building a gymnasium, and what started as a small infection in his hand ballooned into a raging and insidious sepsis, nearly killing him in the process. I mention this because it was so significant in his life and in ours, and we all worried and prayed for him for weeks, him teetering between life and death, and all of us praying without ceasing for his recovery. He did indeed recover, but the healing was incessantly long and his mind was oddly wracked with the realness of his imaginings during his hospital stay, and it seemed to take a toll on him in the ensuing few years. That said, I bring this story to bear for two reasons. One, because my Dad took this illness in stride like he did most things. He was a steady presence through everything in his life. He never seemed to get too high or too low, but rather took each life event and did his best. I really think Joe Bliffen always did his best, and that left a mark on me. The second reason is because of the church. The church loved him through that illness and took care of my Mom and my sister. The body of Christ showed love with casseroles and visits and prayers and patience. The example of love through action took hold of me so viscerally during that time, I knew that the way I loved people would be through action. My Dad showed love through action to others, and the body of Christ showed love to my Dad through action. Words are easy to use. My Dad used words and actions, and I loved him for saying what he meant and doing what he said he would do.

After my Dad's illness in the early 90s, I believe he became restless and his mind was pained. There's no easy way to say what I will say next, but through an excruciating and devastating year for our family, filled with confusion, regret, anger, pain, and silence, our parents divorced, and my Dad moved out of the house with little fanfare. After a year or so spent lying low, he began preaching at a Disciples of Christ Church in about 1999, and here found a home among this unfamiliar and sometimes too progressive for him family of God. The atmosphere here was much different...he was preaching in downtown Columbus on Fourth Street where the vibe was definitely not the suburban thrum that he was accustomed to hearing, but instead was now surrounded by an unfamiliar inner-city buzz. I don't think I can say that my Dad thrived in this environment, but he seemed to eventually have found his rhythm in the church and came to love many people who attended. He would speak often and fondly of his homosexual friend who was the music director at the church, and of his atheist friend who never budged from his beliefs but was seen sitting in a pew every Sunday morning without fail. My Dad found himself among folks who were uncommon to him, who may have taught him something of grace and of love. He was striking a balance between Biblical truths and loving people where they were, and I think he did an outstanding job of both.

It was during this time that Dad remarried. His wife's name was Sara, and in the remarrying, he became a stepparent to two teenaged boys, Heath and Levi. I didn't spend a lot of time with my dad during these years, but it seemed to me that my dad had found a place where he could quietly live his life. I don't think it was comfortable necessarily...I think the pains of the prior years had taken their toll on him, but I will say that in his later years of life he spoke less of legalism and more of grace, and I can say that made me all the more his daughter. While we were not close, I watched him from afar, seeing him every year or every other year, and each visit was an easy, relaxed and familiar gathering. He seemed to have settled into the choices he had made, and while I don't think he ever truly reconciled it in his mind, I know his love for God grew exponentially in those years.

Over the next ten years or so, my dad found a pace that worked for him. He had two dogs, Seven and Soda that he loved, and spent a lot of time in the Outer Banks, sitting on the beach under an umbrella, reading some conspiracy novel or another. His church did not seem to be growing, but it didn't seem to be dwindling either. He seemed satisfied with that arrangement. He continued his ever-diligent study of God's Word, and he would faithfully call me every other week to check in with me. Living close to my sister Devon, he would frequently babysit my niece and nephew Sydney and Andrew, and I grow tears thinking about the care and love he gave to them. He loved his grandkids, and again, his love in action spoke louder than any words ever could.

In March 2014, when Dad was 70, we received the news that he had been diagnosed with Stage IV pancreatic cancer. How could this be? My dad was the vision of health. He wasn't medicated for anything, was a healthy weight, and exercised. But sometimes life throws you ugly things, and you have to deal with them. Over the next twelve weeks, Devon, his wife Sara, his brother, my Uncle John, his friends Carrie and Don, and I shared the load of caring for our Dad as his health dwindled. At first Dad was his usual self, reserved, dry, cracking a little joke here and there, and incessantly watching Don Imus and Jimmy Kimmel on cable. As his health deteriorated, he added House of Cards from Netflix into the mix, and he insisted that we all watch this show with him as he pointed out scenes from the show that he knew would be coming next, so often had he watched the series on a loop. He would doze in and out while the show would grind one into the next, and one of us would always be sitting by to fetch water, medicine, or a mini-ice cream cone for him, as this was the only food he eventually would take.

The spring rapidly rolled into summer and in the final weeks, Dad became more and more withdrawn, spindly, thinner, sicker, and...distilled, I guess. His mind seemed clear most of the time, and when he would catch my eye from his newly installed hospice bed in the living room, sometimes it was more than I could bear to hold his gaze even for a brief second or two. But in those moments, those moments that our eyes locked, I knew that he was okay. That we were okay as a father and daughter who had not been close for a long time, but that this was bigger than that. That he wasn't afraid to die. I knew that it pained him to leave all of us, his family and friends, his dogs, his church, but his eyes showed a quiet confidence that held no fear. He knew where he was going to be after his breath left his body.

My dad died on July 2, 2014 just three months after his diagnosis. I wasn't there when he passed, but during my last visit with him I had the chance to tell him goodbye. It wasn't in so many words, but in actions. I hope that the weeks that I spent caring for him, preparing his food, listening to his stories, and sitting with him was the love in action that he needed. As I think back on those weeks of caring for him, we all loved him into his death, much the same way he loved life into the churches where he preached. The hands and feet of Jesus. The heart and soul of a circle of friends and family. I think that's where heaven and earth met as he passed.

I'm sorry for a lot of things when it comes to my Dad. I'm sorry I didn't spend more time with him in his later years. I'm sorry I didn't ask him more questions about his life and about his family when his mind was solid. I'm sorry I didn't go to church when he preached. He was a wise and fine preacher. I'm sorry he never got to see the end of House of Cards. He would have loved the ending. But mostly I'm sorry that he hasn't gotten to see Devon and me and how we have thrived and succeeded through the total devastation of fire, divorce, breast cancer, poverty, and to see how both our families have risen so high and made wonderful lives for ourselves. His grandkids are all beautiful, smart, driven, and well behaved. His daughters are sassy but hard working. His sons-in-law love their wives and take good care of their families. And remember when I was talking about love in action? Well, I can tell you right now that the Bliffen-Simpson-Menix family group know all about love in action. The hands and feet of Jesus and the heart of a family. A meeting of heaven and earth. I think he'd be proud.

Bob and Jane Bender family
Row 1 – Jane, Mari, Morgan
Row 2 – Martin, Marshall, Melissa, Bob

Chapter 11

MY SISTER, CAROL JANE
BENDER BURKETT
BY JANE BURKETT AND JERRY BLIFFEN

Carol Jane Bliffen was born January 10, 1952, in Charleston, WV, while Dad was preaching at Eskdale. She graduated from Prichard High School, Grayson, Kentucky in 1969. That summer our family moved to Atlanta, Georgia, and she enrolled at Kentucky Christian College. There she met her future husband, Robert "Bob" Bender, from Navarre, Ohio [near Canton]. Bob became the president of the senior class of KCC for the school year 1972-73. Together, Bob and Jane graduated from KCC in May of 1973, and were married June 16, 1973, at the Downtown Christian Church in Johnson City, Tennessee, where Dad was preaching. The following paragraphs were written primarily by Jane.

"Our life together and ministry began at the Dry Run Christian Church outside of Portsmouth, Ohio in April of 1973. The church's stated ministry was to help young preachers get started. We were set up in a little shotgun house next to the church. The house had three rooms with a kitchen/bathroom add on. In the backyard stood a working three-hole outhouse! Bob was paid $90 per week. He was paid in cash from the weekly offerings, and if there was not enough, the church treasurer made up the difference. Our time at Dry Run was a good time to learn about ministry and to figure out about married life. During our first year we began our family with our sweet baby, Mari. She was born in Portsmouth on November 27, 1974. Less than one year later, our second child, Marshall, was born on October 29, 1975. When Marshall was on the way, Bob asked for a $20 raise. When the church felt they could not afford this, we began looking for another position. We even looked into a church in New Zealand. It is a great story of how the Lord said absolutely not!

In December 1975, we took our two babies and moved to an apartment in Newark, Delaware. The Meadowood Christian Church was a split from a church in the area. We met in a YMCA which required set up and tear down every week. Our first Christmas there was the loneliest we had ever been. We did not know the people, and our family was far away. Our ministry there was not successful, but it was the right place to be when Melissa was born. "Missy" was born June 26, 1977 in Wilmington, Delaware. Her feet were severely turned in requiring immediate therapy. A.I. DuPont Hospital for Children is located in Wilmington, which was very convenient. They took care of her and charged only what we could afford. At the beginning of 1978, two of our leading families were transferred out of town, which was our incentive to begin to look elsewhere. Dear friends from Portsmouth had relocated in Pittsburgh, PA, so they recommended us to the Norwin Christian Church. As Providence would have it, one of the elders there was family to my childhood friends.

We began our ministry at Norwin in June of 1978. The church was made up mostly of young families, which made for an excellent situation for our family. (My older children still keep in contact with friends from there). Our housing at Norwin began with a rental from one of the elders. This arrangement made Bob nervous, so we bought the first house that we could afford (a fixer upper before it was popular). While we were there, Martin was born on January 25, 1979, in Pittsburgh. Three years later on April 4, 1982, our fifth child, Morgan, was born. During our 9 ½ years at Norwin, the church grew and was able to build an education and office building. We stayed there until the end of 1987, when Bob's mother developed cancer for the third time.

In January 1988, we moved to the Danville Church of Christ in Ohio to be closer to Bob's mother. The town was glad to see us because we raised the school population by 1%, which meant more money for the school! It was nice to be in a small town where the kids could walk to all their activities and listen for the carillon bells to know when to come home. Being close to family afforded us valuable time with Bob's mother until she passed away in August of 1989. Providence allowed me to be with her as her spirit went to heaven. This would be so important to me later on.

Even though we had promised the children that we would not move again, the Lord made an unmistakable call to the Parkway Christian Church in Sarasota, Florida. We moved there in the summer of 1991. Because this was a new church plant, I needed to go to work in order to help make ends meet. I took a job as office administrator at Faith Christian School which began my career in private Christian schools. During our ministry at Parkway the church grew and became independent. Our children graduated from Bradenton high schools and went on to attend Florida Christian College in Kissimmee.

In 2000 it was time to move again. We began our ministry at First Church of Christ in Eustis, Florida on January 2. My Dad had been the minister there for eight years back in the 1980s. The church family welcomed us with open arms. On September 27, 2002, Bob and I were in a terrible car accident. Bob broke his hip, and I broke my arm, but the Lord graced us both with complete recoveries. During our ministry at Eustis, the church changed her name to Lake Eustis Christian Church in order to avoid confusion with the Orange Avenue Church of Christ [non-instrumental] about a mile away on the same street. Also, we began a second morning worship service, and our historic building was remodeled. I taught at Blue Lake Academy, then later at Adventure Christian Academy. In the fall of 2010, Bob developed pneumonia. He would get better for a time and then it would come back even worse. After several weeks in the hospital in the spring of 2011, Bob went home to be with the Lord on April 16. His remains are interned in the church yard at Lake Eustis.

As of this writing, Bob has been gone for 10 years. In that time, I have experienced the grace of Jesus in miraculous ways. He allowed Bob to live to be 60, so that I would qualify to receive survival benefits from Social Security. According to my budget, I should not have been able to make ends meet, but I not only lived, but thrived! He sent family and friends to love and care for me. Then my parents came to live with me in 2015. I met a widower in our church, Ed Burkett, a retired power company worker from Pennsylvania, around 2014. We began dating and were married on June 18, 2016. He has been a wonderful blessing to me the last few years. My Dad and I were the primary caregivers for my mother the last part of her life. We both were with her when she left our house to dwell in the house of the Lord forever on September 28, 2019. The Lord has certainly been good to me and has always provided for all our needs."

The Bender children have all grown up to be faithful servants of the Lord. They are all happily married to Christian spouses and have at least two children each. In fact, Jane now has 14 grandchildren! As of this writing, Mari's husband, Mark Gaeta, ministers in DeLeon Springs, Florida. Missy's husband, Kasey Kuyper, ministers in Jasper, Georgia. Martin Bender ministers in Glenville, Georgia. All three are serving in our brotherhood of Independent Christian Churches. Marshall is an attorney, and Morgan is a counselor, both living in Southwest Florida. We are all very pleased and thankful for the five Bender children who are shining a bright light for Jesus Christ in their communities where they serve. The faith of the parents is still living in their children and grandchildren!

Jerry D. Bliffen family
Sheila, Sarah, Jerry, Bethany

Chapter 12

My Story, Jerry David and Sheila Bliffen
By Jerry and Sheila Bliffen

In 1971, I was a 16-year-old junior at Headland High School in East Point, Georgia. Surprisingly, one day we had a school assembly program in our gymnasium featuring a contemporary Christian singing group. This was amazing to me, as school sponsored Bible reading and prayer had been expelled from public schools in 1962. Nevertheless, the leader of the group spoke between songs and one statement he made was, "John 3:16 is the only verse from the Bible you need to know." Of course, I knew John 3:16, but I did not think it was the only verse in the Bible I needed to know! For there are more terms of pardon than those contained in any one verse. Though I was not highly intelligent, God gave me enough common sense to question that if John 3:16 was the only verse I needed to know, why did He give us the rest of the Bible? I still think that is a fair question.

About that same time, I was invited to an inter-denominational youth meeting at a large house not far from where I lived. The youth meeting was a weekly Thursday night gathering called "Ranch." The meetings involved group singing, and a Bible study led by a recent graduate, Robert, of Florida Bible College (a "faith only" school in Orlando.). His brief Bible study was followed by an invitation, encouraging sinners to raise their hands if they wanted to be saved. After Robert prayed, young people rejoiced that their friends had "gotten saved" that night. I had been saved since the age of eight when I was baptized into Christ in a revival at the First Church of Christ, Grayson, Kentucky. Palmer Young was the revival evangelist, and John Samples, our associate minister, baptized me and several others on that Tuesday night. (My dad was out of town that evening.) Being raised in the Church of Christ, I had not been exposed to the false teaching I was hearing at "Ranch." I approached Robert and asked him about baptism. He said they would have a big baptismal service in the spring in the swimming pool, but baptism had nothing to do with salvation. He proceeded to show me several Scripture verses that involve being saved by grace through faith that did not mention baptism. I was open-minded and confused so I went home and talked to my Dad about these verses, and Dad explained to me the fact that faith involved the action of obedience which included baptism. I went back to Robert and talked to him again, but he again gave me more verses and reasons why baptism was not essential to salvation. I ended up asking Robert to come to our house and discuss salvation with my Dad. Both were willing, so Robert came one evening and they discussed the Scriptures and the plan of salvation for well over an hour. When the evening was over, neither one had a changed mind, but I knew where I stood! I had been open and willing to change my belief, but that discussion sealed the fact that I had *not* been misled all my life. Salvation is by grace through faith...grace includes all God has done for us to save us, and faith includes all we do to receive His grace...including baptism into Christ. Dad won the debate decisively! I never went back to the "Ranch" meetings again. But from that time on, I was even more determined to go to KCC and study the Bible. I have always believed the Bible is God's Holy Word and the most important book one could ever study. What in this world could possibly be more important than knowing and doing what God has said? I still think that is a fair question as well.

Before living in Georgia, we lived for 10 years in Grayson, KY. Growing up on the campus of KCC was a wonderful blessing! My best friends were children of other professors, and I enjoyed talking with students at the college and attending special events on campus. It was really special watching my uncles, John and Joe, as well as many others play basketball for the Knights. I knew I wanted to do that as well, and later, I did!

Most of the college students were busy with their work and extra-curricular activities and had little time to devote to professors' kids. But there were two students who were especially nice to us, Bob Werntz and Johnny Johnson. Bob later ministered in Pike County, married one of Sheila's best friends, Betty, and sang at our wedding. Our friendship continues to this day. Johnny was raised at Mountain Mission School, in Grundy Virginia and worked on the college farm. He would take my friends and me fishing at the college pond—even baiting and taking the fish off the hooks! My wife would later be a teacher at MMS were my friend Johnny had grown up. The story of MMS is an amazing story of the power and provision of the mighty God we serve!

In the summers, Professor Tom Gemeinhart, our neighbor, would invite all of the neighborhood to play volleyball many evenings after supper. It was so much fun playing with the grown-ups and having some very competitive games. "Mr. G" always played to win, and so did I!

Another tremendous blessing in my life while growing up in Grayson was the opportunity to attend Ruby Maggard's kindergarten class at the First Church of Christ. She was a wonderful and loving teacher! During that year she had us memorize Luke 2:1-20, which we quoted at our Christmas program. In the spring we quoted the 23rd Psalm at our kindergarten graduation. We all received a New Testament with our name engraved on the front cover.

In the summer of 1969, we moved from Grayson to Atlanta, Georgia. It was a difficult transition for my brothers and me, as we had to make new friends in a large city after having lived in small-town USA for 10 years. However, we did adjust. We made friends, and I became Co-Vice President of my senior class. I learned to drive on Atlanta's freeways, worked part-time at a Putt-Putt golf course and cut weeds with a swing blade for the city of East Point. After graduating from Headland High School, I left Georgia and traveled with my sister to attend KCC in the fall of 1972. The foothills of the Bluegrass State welcomed me, and I felt like I had come home. My freshman year was quite eventful as I met my future wife, being introduced to her in the old cafeteria lunch line by her ex-boyfriend and my roommate, Roger Breeding. Roger was from the Elkhorn City Church of Christ, and Sheila was from the Coal Run Church of Christ, both in Pike County. Little did I know then that one day I would serve both of those churches (most recently as a fill-in preacher at Elkhorn City). By October of our first semester, Sheila and I were sweethearts, and that has continued to this day. My college years were filled with classes, term papers, study, work, basketball, ministries, and of course, dates and meals with Sheila!

On our first date alone, I borrowed a car from a married couple from the Coal Run Church who were also students at KCC, Ronnie and Linda Abshire. I drove Sheila to Ashland where we ate at Frisch's and visited her Grandmother Cora and Aunt Earlene (E.W.'s mother and sister.) Ronnie and Linda have been our good friends for almost 50 years. In fact, I would say Ronnie is the most outstanding "Timothy" the Coal Run Church ever produced. E.W. Damron baptized Ronnie and Linda on June 28, 1970, and Coal Run gave financial support to Ronnie and Linda during their college years. He began preaching at the Grays Chapel Christian Church, (Beattyville, Kentucky) in August 1972. He later served the Macon (Ohio) Church of Christ, the Hardy (Kentucky) Church of Christ, the Sandhill Church of Christ (South Shore, Kentucky,) the Crooked Creek Church of Christ (Peach Creek, West Virginia,) the Grandview Christian Church (Beaver, West Virginia,) the First Christian Church (Babson Park, Florida,) the Manila Church of Christ, (Chapmanville, West Virginia,) and the Glyn Lyn Church of Christ (Virginia). Ronnie has had success in all of his many ministries for nearly 50 years, serving in five different states. At this writing, Ronnie is 72 years old, and is enjoying a return ministry at Babson Park.

After our sophomore year, Sheila and I were 20 years old and wanted to get married. We had saved enough money to buy an 8 x 42 trailer on campus that we purchased from Ken Beck (a future president of St. Louis Christian College.) My Dad helped make it possible for us to tie the knot by giving us the 1967 Buick he had allowed me to drive to get to my ministries in Pike County. We married on August 17, 1974 at the Coal Run Church where Sheila's father, E.W. Damron, ministered. Both of our fathers had a part in the ceremony. It was a beautiful wedding. Sheila's Mother, Mary and her Aunt May Crum made her wedding dress. Several ladies in the church helped with wedding plans and all that summer it was the hot topic every evening. I even cleaned the windows of the church on the outside to get ready for the big event!

During my college years I preached for the Shelby Church of Christ in 1973. In 1974, I was the weekend youth minister for the Zebulon Church of Christ under Bill Ford, minister. In the summer of 1974, I began teaching Junior Church at the Pikeville Church of Christ, where Bob Werntz was the minister. I would teach the High School Sunday School class at Zebulon, then drive to Pikeville 15 minutes away and teach Junior Church. I then led youth meeting at 6 PM before the evening service at Zebulon. In January 1975, I became youth minister at Coal Run, while continuing to teach Junior Church at Pikeville. The Pikeville Church of Christ had been started around 1971 by members of Coal Run, Zebulon, and the Fords Branch Churches of Christ. I enjoyed serving both churches until July 1976, when I began my first full-time ministry in Vansant, Virginia.

Two of my favorite professors in Bible college were Don Nash and Tom Gemeinhart. Over their careers, both of these men taught and challenged thousands of young people to preach and teach God's word to a sinful world. "Mr. G." was probably the best Church History and Missions professor in our brotherhood. Don Nash was an outstanding scholar, author, and Bible teacher. I had brother Nash for three years of Greek, and all the New Testament classes I could take under him. I guess you could call me a "Nasharine!" At that time, he used the New American Standard Bible, but sometimes he would disagree with its translation. I once asked him why he didn't make his own translation of the New Testament. He laughed it off, but 25 years later, he did just that— A Literal and Consistent Version of the New Testament. One professor I had for Old Testament did not believe the days of Genesis 1 were literal 24-hour days. I found that out when I wrote a term paper on that very topic. I said the view of seeing the days of Genesis 1 as millions of years was a "liberal view." He wrote on my paper that that was his view, and he did not consider himself a liberal! (If you want more information on Genesis, I recommend "Answers in Genesis", or the Creation Museum in northern Kentucky. But do not accept their plan of salvation, which sadly leaves out baptism, the very place where we gain the benefits of the blood of Christ!) I also enjoyed having Don Nash's son, Francis Nash, for a class on 20th Century History. At that time (1975) the 20th century was only three fourths over! In early 1975, Francis predicted that Jimmy Carter would be elected the next President of the U.S. Having lived in Georgia, (where Carter had been governor) I did not believe that would happen. But needless to say, he was right! Many years later I shared a room with Francis for a week in Queretaro, Mexico while working on a building for the Universidad Christiana de Mexico. As of this writing, Francis continues as the director of Workers for Mexico, an extension of Clinton Looney's work which serves 53 different evangelists and ministries across 12 states of Mexico! He also ministers to Sugar Grove Christian Church near Mt. Sterling where he began his ministry 53 years ago and just recently retired as General Manager of WGOH radio station in Grayson.

I played basketball at KCC for 3 years. My Junior year I had just gotten married, had 2 ministries, worked in the cafeteria, was taking my most difficult classes, and knew I would not get a lot of playing time, so I sat out that year. There were several seniors on the team who would play ahead of me and I just didn't want to sacrifice the time and effort to sit the bench. My senior year I came back to play after losing the 20 pounds I had gained during my time off. We won our first two games, becoming the champions of the KCC Invitational Tournament. This was the highlight of my basketball career! I was so glad my parents and Sheila's parents were both in attendance when we beat Cincinnati Bible Seminary by one point on a last-second shot. I was supposed to get the shot, but since I was double teamed, Cary Lawhon scored from the top of the circle. We only won 3 games the remainder of the season and lost 20. Berea College beat us 3 times: at home by 40 points; at the Centre College Tournament by 50 points; and at Berea by 60 points! Obviously, we had no business playing some of the teams that coach Bob Baird had scheduled. He was a good man and an excellent teacher, but in my opinion, he was not a good coach. At the end of the season, I did receive a trophy for being the team's leading scorer, but I was also the *leading shooter* for the Knights in 1975-76! In 2 different losses on the road, I scored 37 points, but I would have gladly given those points to someone else on our team if only we could have won those games. I still don't like to lose! Just ask my grandsons!

An unusual basketball trip adventure happened one very cold night in the middle of winter, when we lost generator power on our bus. It was about 15° and we were returning from another loss on the road. Fortunately, it was a clear night, and we had a full moon to light our way, because we had *no lights and no heat* on the bus! John Brooks was driving the bus 80 mph on I-64 trying to get us back to Grayson as soon as possible. All the coats we had were blazers that we were required to wear to our away games. I went to sit by Dick Damron, who was our assistant coach (and Sheila's boss for three years, working as his secretary). We were both freezing, but we found a black garbage bag to put our legs in, to try to stay warm. Coach Damron made the comment, "I always wanted to spend the night in a trash bag with Jerry Bliffen!" Our bus was soon pulled over by the Kentucky State Police, and John got out to explain our situation. The police officer told John to get back on the bus, and he would lead us back to our campus. So, we continued on I-64 at 80 mph, following a police car with blue lights flashing. "The stately walls of KCC" never looked so good as they did that night when we finally got back to campus. The following year Dick Damron became the head basketball coach. He was blessed to have some talented freshmen to lead his team to success. I do not believe Dick Damron ever had a losing season during his tenure as coach. In fact, he led the Knights to several national championships! Oh, how I wish Dick could have been my coach!

Sheila and I graduated from KCC May 7, 1976. Sheila graduated Magna Cum Laude and with a PHT degree ("putting hubby through!"). She certainly earned that honor, as she typed every writing assignment I ever turned in all four years! After graduation, I was interviewed by the Sebring (Ohio) Church of Christ and preached a trial sermon for a youth ministry position there. The next Sunday I preached a trial message at the Vansant Church of

Christ for the preaching ministry there. Both churches voted for me on the same day and invited me to come. After much prayer and consideration, we decided to move to Vansant.

I was ordained to the ministry on June 20, 1976 at Coal Run. Both my Dad and my father-in-law, E.W. had a part in the service, as well as Bob Werntz, who sang "I was Born to Serve the Lord." The elders were Sherwood Cool, Charlie Chaffins, and Eugene King. Many years later I preached the funeral of both Sherwood and Eugene. Before I began my ministry at Vansant, David McVeigh was serving as the interim preacher. We shared the pulpit in the month of July and worked together in the community. In August he went to Ozark Christian College in Joplin, Missouri to further his study for ministry. My first Sunday was the bicentennial of our nation, July 4, 1976. Many men of the church sported full beards for the bicentennial, and then shaved them off sometime after the 4th. On my second Sunday, July 11, my audience look totally different! And actually, many of the men looked better with a beard!

In 1976, Vansant had no parsonage, so the church rented us an apartment in a junkyard on Slate Creek, about 1 ½ miles from MMS. It was a second-floor apartment with red sulfur water that we could not drink or use for laundry. When we took a bath, it would turn our skin a reddish color. We were certainly thankful when in 1977, the church bought a house next to the Presbyterian Church in Vansant that became the parsonage we lived in until 1990. We still had red sulfur water from a well, so I laid a 2-inch plastic pipe in a spring nearby and would siphon water into a basement storage tank. The water was then pumped into the house. At least it was clear and we could do laundry and bathe without turning our skin red! How happy we were when the county finally installed water lines and we had "city water!"

The church was blessed with slow, but steady growth as I learned more and more about ministry through experience and many godly mentors. My mentors in ministry included my Dad, my father-in-law, E.W., Clarence Greenleaf, Mike Trent, Jim Viers, and Clinton Looney. My life has been truly blessed by these men of faith who were my family, friends, coworkers, examples, and encouragers!

Ministry at Vansant involved planning for three services a week, Sunday school lessons, Vacation Bible Schools, many weeks of camp at the Church of Christ Youth Camp, the National Prayer Clinic, teaching at Grundy Bible Institute, revival meetings, missionary rallies, Crusades for Christ, and a daily 15-minute radio broadcast on WNRG in Grundy at 9:30 AM (one week every 6 to 8 weeks.) It also involved hundreds of fellowship meals, hospital visits, home visits, and funerals. A death in the mountains would often involve two evening services, the funeral and graveside service. It usually also involved a meal to be prepared and taken to the family or served at the church building. It was always a stressful and time-consuming event for me. But it also afforded many opportunities to share the good news of Jesus with people who were hurting and needing to hear some good news. Funerals are a wonderful opportunity to meet more people and meet their deepest need during a time of grief.

One time I preached the funeral of a man who had made his confession of faith to me in the hospital, but soon totally lost his mind as blood clots were racing through his body. He died the next day at a hospital 75 miles away before ever having been immersed. His was a difficult funeral to preach... basically, I just preached the gospel. Not long after that, his brother had a heart attack while working in a coal mine. He was rushed to the hospital and wanted to be baptized. After dealing with an unbelieving doctor, I baptized the small man into Christ in a therapy tank that was only meant for the lower body. He still had coal dust on his body as he was immersed, face forward, not to put off the dirt of the body, but to cleanse his soul, having his sins washed away. He was then put into ICU, but he fully recovered and became a faithful member of the Vansant Church of Christ.

Another coal miner I baptized was dying in the Grundy Hospital with lung disease. Johnny Nichols wanted to be baptized, but there was no tank or tub in the hospital large enough in which to immerse him. I arranged for the Grundy Funeral Home (owned by Junior Mullins of the Grundy church) to bring a burial vault to the hospital. We turned it upside-down and filled it with warm water we carried down the hall in buckets to his room. It was not convenient for man, but it was obedient to God. Three weeks later his body was buried again, but his spirit went to heaven.

One other memorable conversion was that of Henry Effler, the oldest man I ever baptized. He was 89 years old and died about three months after he was converted. He is another man who came to Christ in the 11th hour of life.

Some very pleasant memories from our 14 years at Vansant were the Sunday nights after church going to eat with several couples from the church. We many times went to Burger Queen, Druthers, or the Rainbow Restaurant where we would eat, laugh, and fellowship together. We also shared in many fellowship meals following Sunday night services at church. There were also many occasions we were invited to the home of Red and Mary Cook where we shared some good popcorn and a delicious piece of cake, made by Mary Lee. On every occasion, the food was good, but the fellowship was better!

On March 6, 1980, Sheila and I were blessed with the birth of our first daughter, Bethany Dianne. She was healthy overall, but did have a very colicky stomach, and several ear infections until we found out her ears were not producing wax. For a long time, we had to put eardrops in her ears every day. If Bethany had been a boy, her name would've been "Benjamin Joseph." Many years later, Bethany would go to China and adopt a 12-year-old boy and give him the English name, "Benjamin." Bethany was a beautiful baby, and filled our family with love and laughter, pride and joy. Two and one-half years later, our second daughter, Sarah Ruth, was born August 5, 1982. Sheila gave birth without the epidural block, which was used to prevent the extreme pain of childbirth. After Sarah was born, Sheila informed me that if we had any more children, I would have them. Since "I know nothing about birthin' babies," Sarah was our last child and completed our family! Sarah was healthier than Bethany, in that all she did for a year, it seemed, was eat and sleep. Bethany and Sarah grew up as best friends and good girls, but with totally different personalities. Bethany was baptized into Christ at seven years of age during a Crusade for Christ in July 1987 when her favorite song happened to be the invitation hymn, "People Need the Lord." Sarah wanted to be baptized when she was only six years of age. We told her she needed to wait until she was seven, so for several months she would say "I cannot wait until my seventh birthday when I can be baptized." About a month before her seventh birthday (1989), Sheila asked me if we were doing the right thing in making her wait until she was seven. How much more would she know in one month's time? She knew the gospel and saw the need to have her sins forgiven. So, at that time we told her she did not have to wait until she was seven, and the next time we had church, she could come forward and I would baptize her. The very next Sunday morning, my six-year-old daughter walked the aisle, confessed her faith in Jesus, was baptized, and was the happiest little girl I have ever seen! She has been faithful to her Lord ever since.

Both of our daughters graduated from Pike County Central High School with a 4.0 GPA. They both were awarded 4-year academic scholarships to Pikeville College, and graduated debt free. What a tremendous blessing to our family! Bethany was Valedictorian of her college class, and she was pregnant with our first granddaughter as she walked across the stage to receive her diploma on that momentous occasion. Both Bethany and Sarah have gone on to receive their Masters' Degrees and are National Board-Certified Teachers of mathematics. They are married to Christian husbands (Chad and Matt), and all four of them work in the field of public education. Bethany has five children and three stepchildren. Two of Bethany's children were adopted from China. Her children are Alyson, Luke, Elijah, Lydia, and Benjamin. Her stepchildren are Blake, Blair, and Bree Thompson. Sarah has two boys, Jay and Jonah. We love our ten grandchildren dearly and spend as much time as possible supporting them in their many activities and having fun together. My quiver is full, and I am blessed! [Psalm 127:5 KJV]

Sheila has had some part-time jobs but was primarily "a stay at home" mother, wife, and servant of the churches. When Sarah was ready to enter kindergarten, Sheila was invited to teach fifth grade at Mountain Mission School. So, in August 1988, Sheila began her teaching career in the most challenging environment a new elementary teacher could imagine. She was warned in advance that this group was a tough group, but she had no idea just how tough her job would be. On her class roll were 24 students, 18 boys and 6 girls. Of those students, many were older than the normal 5th grader. You see, many of these children were Hispanics who could barely speak English or didn't know English at all. The language barrier was difficult. The age difference was difficult. And some of the children were just not well adjusted because of their upbringing and unfortunate circumstances in life before coming to Mountain Mission School. Sheila would come home some nights and cry because her heart was hurting for her students. Other nights she would cry because she was so frustrated with their behavior. She was once called "a big old, little old, black Ethiopian" when she made a student wash the wall where he had written dirty words. With a smile on her face she replied, "James, I believe you are color blind." James was African/American! But the positive far outweighed the negative that year! She worked hard in planning lessons, grading papers, loving students, and teaching all subjects except Science. Once their Science teacher, Steve Barnett, had the students make terrariums. They were all lined up in the window seals of the 5th grade classroom. Steve's son, Rick, had caught a little green snake and put in his terrarium. It was only covered with a piece of paper, held on by a rubber band. One morning, the students informed "Mrs. Bliffen" that the snake was missing. One of the boys had put a hole in the paper cover the day before so the snake could escape. Sheila hates snakes, and was quite upset, but tried not to alarm the students. They looked around the classroom, but the snake was not to be found. At the first restroom break, Sheila let the six girls go back to the classroom while she waited in the hallway for the 18 boys. She heard a scream from the girls and knew they had seen the snake. In fact, the snake was crawling out of the heat register! That little green creature of God was immediately returned to its' home in the great outdoors.

From that class of 5th graders, Sheila has been able to reconnect with many of them through Facebook. Some of their professions today are Doctor, Chiropractor, Nurse Anesthetist, Bank Officer and Social Worker. Their successes bring her so much joy. She treasures the memories of her first year of teaching at Mountain Mission School. At the end of that year, Sheila had decided to retire from her 1-year teaching career but was offered the best class in the elementary school, 3rd grade, if she would stay the next year, so she did. That class proved to be a joy to her, and our daughter, Bethany was in that group. Having her child in class had both positive and negative aspects. Bethany was an excellent student, and it was a joy for Sheila to watch her learn. But it was difficult for her to allow Bethany any privileges that would appear that she was favoring her daughter. However, Bethany did get the leading part in the 3rd grade school play! All in all, it was a great year of learning for some awesome children.

During her years at Mountain Mission, Sheila had health problems, probably stemming from allergies. She had walking pneumonia several times, but never missed a day of teaching. After a scary episode that required her to be hospitalized, I decided she had to give up her job. By this time, she was in her third year of teaching. She was heartbroken, upset and became very depressed. But I felt it was necessary to get her healthy again. That was in December of 1989. In the summer of 1990, we moved to Coal Run. Sheila's years teaching at Mountain Mission School are some of her best memories in her Christian service and she is so thankful to have had that opportunity.

While Sheila was working at Mountain Mission, I would often eat lunch in the cafeteria with her, our daughters, and other MMS children at her table. They always had a good, nutritious meal and it was a joy to be in the company of the staff and children. Sheila and I became friends of most of the staff and have always respected their dedication to the Lord and those precious children from around the world! We were asked to move on campus and work full-time, but I did not have enough dedication to work 24/7 with almost no free time to do anything else. I have often said the staff at Mountain Mission is over worked and under paid, yet they have had the joy of watching thousands of children grow into outstanding Christian adults. I did serve as volunteer assistant basketball coach in 1988, under coach Jim Thompson (who had previously served under me as youth minister while he was a student at Kentucky Christian College.) I also refereed many games to help out. Special friends at Mountain Mission are Ernie and Patti Hertzog who came to MMS in 1972 and have used their many talents there for almost 50 years. One of their 2 sons is working there today. Ernie and I try to get together once a week during good weather to play golf, along with another good Mountain Mission staff friend, Steve Barnett. Once when we lived at Vansant, Sheila prepared a nice meal for Ernie and Patti, I made a fire in the fireplace, and I had told Ernie to leave their boys with someone and he and Patti could enjoy an evening alone at our house. We got everything ready and left for several hours. When we returned, they were still there and had brought their boys! They had thoroughly enjoyed the evening.

A very important part of my ministry in the 70s, 80s, 90s, and 2000s was working at the Church of Christ Youth Camp every summer and serving at the camp in some capacity at the National Prayer Clinic every October. The first time I ever went to camp was to help as a team leader and teacher under E.W. Damron, who was the camp Dean. Going up that steep, winding, narrow, dirt road outside of Vansant to the top of Baldwin Mountain was a unique experience in itself. But when reaching the top of the mountain, everything opened up to a beautiful campus with incredible views of God's handiwork in Southwest Virginia. The first weeks of camp ever held were in 1969, with E.W. Damron and Jim Viers working together as Dean and Assistant Dean for both senior and junior weeks. Sheila and I were blessed to work with both of these wonderful men of God. We have had some outstanding weeks of camp working with many dedicated men and women of God. Our hard-working camp manager was Larry Fields, a deacon at Vansant. He and his wife Sandy worked alongside her mother, Polly Kennedy, who was our camp cook for many years. They made the camp a wonderful, beautiful place of love, joy, and good food! In those summer weeks of camp, we were blessed with a lot of happy campers who decided to follow Jesus during those wonderful times at the CCYC! I had the opportunity to serve with E.W. for several years as his Assistant Dean, and then later served as Dean for Junior, Intermediate, Junior High, and Senior weeks of camp ....as well as a few Family camps. We especially enjoyed working with the Gaminde family from Abingdon for several summers in the 80's when we would have at least 20-35 decisions for Christ in one week! One summer we baptized over 25 young people from Vansant alone, and immediately saw the need to hire a youth minister. One year we had the singing group "Tribute" work with us at camp which involved my two brothers, Jim and John, and my cousin, Tom

Thomas. That was a special week! I served as co-chairman of the National Prayer Clinic for many years and became the Chairman in 2015 and continue to plan this annual gathering at the camp.

One of the most outstanding high school students at Vansant when we first started our ministry there was Mike Rife. He was 16, and we were 22. We quickly became friends, and that friendship continues to this day. Mike would spend many hours at our house, and we enjoyed every moment of his visits. After graduating from Grundy High School, he was planning to play baseball at Emory and Henry College, but we encouraged him to go to Kentucky Christian College. It was on the last night of Senior week that summer at CCYC, when he went forward at the invitation hymn and announced he was going to KCC! We were thrilled! Mike played baseball at KCC and became one of the most unforgettable students of the 70s-80s. He bought our daughter, Bethany, a Yankees helmet when she was a little girl and brainwashed her into becoming a Yankees fan! We forgave him because he went into the ministry and has been a very successful preacher! After the deaths of Clarence Greenleaf and Mike Trent, he was the Chairman of the National Prayer Clinic for several years. Mike followed me at Vansant in 1990 and has been the preacher of his home church for over 31 years. The church has thrived during his ministry. He is definitely the best "Timothy" Vansant has ever produced! God's providence is now clearly evident in Mike's decision on that last night of Sr. Week at CCYC.

During our ministry at Vansant, Sheila was very involved in the work. She played the piano and organ for services and for the choir, and she recruited Mary Beth (Merricks) Stiltner and Donna (Smith) Fletcher to play as well. She taught youth classes and directed many musicals for the children. She helped to start a weekly ladies' group, "Sonshine Servants," who met to fellowship and make quilts. She and Betty Shields planned the very first Ladies Day at CCYC. The ladies at Vansant Church of Christ were very active and were wonderful mentors to my young wife. When we started our ministry at Vansant, we were very inexperienced, but God provided men and women there who were exemplary in service and leadership. Those precious people are friends forever!

After 14 years at the Vansant Church of Christ, we moved to Coal Run to begin our ministry there on July 1, 1990. E.W. was 65 years old and was retiring from full time ministry. I was 36 years old and very happy and excited to move back to Kentucky and begin serving the church where I had been ordained and had served as youth minister. E.W. had begun the ministry of East Kentucky Bible Institute in 1969, so he asked me to become President of EKBI. For many years EKBI had classes in 5 to 6 different churches of Christ in Pike County. Our class at Coal Run met on Monday nights from 7- 8:30 PM. We would usually have from 10- 20 students in our class. Classes would begin in mid-September and would conclude the end of March. EKBI would today be called a small group ministry/Bible college night class. It afforded a wonderful time of spiritual growth, fellowship, and training for service for many Christians.

When we moved to Coal Run, the Volunteer Fire Department was on the church's property on the riverbank. With it being right behind the parsonage, it was natural that I became a member of the Fire Department. I served for five years, and though I enjoyed the fellowship, I did not enjoy the work or the pressure of having to respond at inopportune times to fires and automobile accidents in our area. When it became mandatory that firemen meet every Tuesday night for training, I decided to resign. At that time, I was teaching on Monday and Wednesday nights, teaching Sunday school, and preaching twice on Sunday. My girls were playing basketball and many of their games were on Tuesday nights. I did not want to miss their games.

In 1990 I began a monthly newsletter, the "Coal Run Caller." It took a lot of time but was a good outreach to our church family both near and far away, as well as informing sister churches of our many ministries, including annual mission trips. Mike Harris helped me with the folding, addressing, and stamping the newsletters. Mike was a disabled coal miner, having broken his back in a roof fall in the late 80's. Though he lived in constant pain, and had to catharize himself to empty his bladder, he was thankful for his accident because he knew he would not be a Christian if it had not happened. He was baptized in 1987 by E.W. and Tony Casebolt, seated in a wooden chair. He was crippled but could walk a little using a cane. Mike had been a great athlete at Mullins High School and loved sports. Though he could not play himself, he coached our church's softball and basketball teams to many winning seasons! All the men who played for Mike loved and respected him tremendously. We wanted to win for him as much as for our team. He kept our stats and the books on every game. I loved playing church league softball, but I loved Mike much more. I was with him and his wife and family in the hospital one day when he was suffering pain like no one I have ever seen. I am so thankful that after suffering pain day and night the entire 17 years of his Christian life, his pain ended at his promotion to heaven on October 2, 2004. I miss his friendship, but I know it will be renewed in glory!

In my ministry at Coal Run, I was privileged to baptize three men who would later become elders in the church, and who continue in that service to this day. Gary Hamilton was converted to Christ on Easter Sunday, April 11, 1993, also my 39th birthday. He and Jerry Nichols responded to the gospel invitation that day and have been faithful members and workers for the Lord. Gary's wife, Diana was a faithful example to him for many years before he made his decision for the Lord. Gary served as a deacon before becoming an elder and teacher. Sadly, Gary lost his wife, Diana suddenly and unexpectedly when she died of a stroke. His grief was great, but God placed Charlene, a wonderful Christian lady in his path that became his wife and helpmate. Gary and Charlene are a great team in service to Christ.

Steve Slone, his wife Sandy and son Josh were baptized on a weekday, March 28, 1996. At the invitation of Diane Hamilton, Gary's wife, the Slone family attended a Fall Festival at the church and from that one function, they started attending services, were converted and immediately became workers in the Kingdom. They have blessed our congregation as faithful leaders, teachers, and especially in tech support. Their daughter, Savannah gave her life to Christ a few years later, and was instrumental in leading her boyfriend (now husband) Nathan Mills to the Lord. Nathan is a deacon and Youth Director at Coal Run. Savannah is a teacher and pianist. The Slone and Mills families are tremendous servants and examples of faithfulness.

On Wednesday night, August 29, 2001, three generations in one family made decisions for the Lord and were baptized into Christ. A teen-age girl,

Sarah Beth Dye, had attended church at Coal Run with her parents for many years, but none of them had given their lives to the Lord. Sarah reached the point that she was ready to make that most important decision. Her decision led to the baptisms of her parents, Steve and LaVerne, her aunt, Shari Cecil, and her grandfather, Bud Dye, all that same night! Bud's wife, Charlene, a long-time member of the church at Coal Run, said of her granddaughter, Sarah Beth, "She looked like an angel stepping into the baptistry!" Years later Sheila and I introduced Sarah Beth to Bryan Goins, son of Jim Goins of the Goins Brothers bluegrass group. They were married and now have two little girls and remain faithful members at Coal Run. Steve Dye became an elder at Coal Run, and his wife, LaVerne became our church treasurer after serving as Mayor of the City of Coal Run Village for eight years. That August night in 2001 was a wonderful and memorable night in my ministry --- just two weeks before a terrible day in our nation, September 11, 2001! I thank God for Gary Hamilton, Steve Slone and Steve Dye, three men who love the Lord, love the Church and serve well as shepherds of the flock at Coal Run.

Another memorable conversion was that of a young Junior High girl, Brittany Carter. Brittany decided to become a Christian while a camper at the Church of Christ Youth Camp. She waited to be baptized on Saturday afternoon after coming home so her family could witness it. At that time, she and her parents and sister had been attending another church. Her sister was a Christian but her parents were not. Immediately after Brittany's baptism, the whole Carter family started attending Coal Run Church of Christ. After a few years both of her parents accepted Christ and became faithful members at Coal Run. Brittany's boyfriend, Jon Lyons made his decision for Christ while working in the kitchen for a week of camp at CCYC. I baptized Jon in the swimming pool at the camp, where many others have been buried with Christ and raised to new life! Today, Brittany and Jon Lyons have two children, Georgia and Oliver (adopted from China). Brittany plays keyboard and sings with the worship team and teaches a class on Wednesday nights. Jon is a deacon, helps with the youth and plays drums with the worship team. Jon is now a Doctor and Brittany is a Music Teacher at John

Creek Elementary. What a blessing the Carter/Lyons families are to the work of Christ at Coal Run!

A long-standing tradition at Coal Run is celebrating our Senior Citizens the last Sunday of October with a special meal after the morning service. Fifty years after the end of WWII, I had the privilege of sitting between two veterans of that war during that wonderful fellowship meal. Wendall Gilliam was in the Army in Berlin, Germany, April of 1945, when the war in Europe ended. J.D. Compton was in the Navy in Toyoko Bay, August of 1945, when Japan finally surrendered. What an honor it was for me to have that meal between these two wonderful veterans. They were just two of several faithful members of our church who had given so much in service to our nation and our Lord! Other WWII veterans from Coal Run included Scott Spradlin, Charles (Duke) Sword, (both of whom were wounded in combat) Jim Kitchen, Eugene King and E.W. Damron. There were probably others that I can't remember, but they all saved our nation from evil tyrants in Japan and Germany who were responsible for the suffering and death of millions throughout the world. Thank God for faithful, humble men of God who gave so much in service to our nation and our Lord! They truly were "The Greatest Generation."

In the ministry at Coal Run, Sheila found her niche in teaching the youth, specifically the teens. She connected well with them and taught their Sunday night class for many years. During that time, she started the Youth Choir. I sang with the guys, helping them learn to sing their harmony part. I was the only bald-headed "boy" in the choir! This group traveled all over our area, singing in sister churches. At one time, there were over 30 kids in the Youth Choir. This work was very fulfilling for Sheila. Many young people gave their lives to Christ during the years the Youth Choir was active. It's a joy to know that many of them are still actively serving the Lord in various places today. The kids in the choir brought in friends to participate and many times won them to Christ. It is important to mention that there were very supportive parents, without whom the Youth Choir would not have been able to travel. Steve Slone was the sound technician, and faithfully served in that capacity as long as the Youth Choir existed. We had to have two buses and other vehicles to transport the youth and equipment and Richie & Susie Phillips, Steve & Debbie Treap, Steve & Sandy Slone and Clarissa Friend were always willing to help and travel with us. God truly blessed this ministry, and we praise Him for the many opportunities the Youth Choir had to share their faith in Christ!

In later years, Sheila led the efforts to start a Praise & Worship Team at Coal Run. It was difficult for her. She had never played this style of music and had to teach herself how to play from chord sheets and lead sheets. The Praise Team used a blend of hymn arrangements and contemporary Christian songs, which made it easier for the congregation to transition without much negative criticism. It really added a new dimension to our worship services and allowed more people the opportunity to use their musical talents to praise God. Toward the end of our ministry, the stress became very difficult for Sheila and she was more than ready to let someone else take over at our retirement. Thankfully we were blessed with Trey Mouton, our new Minister, who was ready and able to lead the Worship Team. Savannah Mills and Brittany Lyons, two of Sheila's former piano students were already stepping in at keyboard and piano when needed, and they were more than willing to assume playing full-time. This brings Sheila and me so much joy to see these young ladies that she taught using their talents for the Lord. I might add, these ladies were also students in Sheila's high school class and now they teach classes and work with our youth. To God be the glory!

Through the span of 30 years Sheila was able to supplement our income by teaching private piano lessons. She would often start students at age 7 or 8 and teach them through high school. One year she had 33 students, teaching five days a week! She enjoyed the one-on-one teaching experience and developed close relationships with many of her students and their parents. Lessons were 30 minutes, and she usually started at 3:00 and taught until 5:30 or 6:00PM. It was nice to be able to work from home. I heard many piano lessons through the years while eating supper and made friends with many of her students.

Through the years our church was able to buy property on both sides of our building. In 20 years, we bought 4 different houses to get more land for our future growth (2 on either side.). We eventually tore the houses down, making room for more parking and a new addition to our building, which would more than double the size of our facility! The church started a building fund in the 2000's, and by 2009 we had saved $800,000 and were ready to build. Goodman Architectural Services in Joplin, Missouri was hired to design our new building. We formed a Building Committee composed of five men and five ladies who worked together very well. The ladies' main responsibility was colors, lights, furniture, and finishing details. I was the chairman of the committee and Steve Treap was hired to be the Construction Manager. We had a ground-breaking service the last of May 2009 and construction began in June. During construction many of our members did a lot of volunteer work throughout the project, including all the painting—a total of 175 gallons! Our first service in the new building was August 15, 2010.

Right in the middle of construction, my father-in-law, E.W. died of a stroke on October 29, 2009 at 84 years of age. Sheila and I immediately became the primary care givers for her mother, Mary. She was handicapped and utilized a power chair but could see to many of her personal needs. There were things she had to have assistance with, for which Sheila and I assumed responsibility. Because it was not safe for her to be alone at night, we would leave the parsonage every evening and spend the night in the house we now live in as an inheritance. It was about this time that I started experiencing trouble with my nerves and had trouble sleeping, but we took it one day at a time. We cared for Mary for 4 1/2 years until she also died of a stroke on March 26, 2014 at age 86. Now they are both in "Glory," one of E.W.'s favorite words. We are looking forward to a wonderful homecoming when we all get to heaven!

After moving into the new auditorium, we needed to remodel the old auditorium into a fellowship hall and kitchen, so by December 2010, we were $900,000 in debt. We had a tremendous special offering for our building on the last Sunday of that November, and Sheila and I gave the largest offering of our lives that day. Three weeks later I received a call from a widow in our church, Helen Ratliff. She asked if I could take her to two banks. She had a Certificate of Deposit mature and she wanted to give it on the church's building debt. It was $130,000, so our debt went down to $770,000 that day! About a month later Helen had a stroke and was in the hospital 23 days. She had no living immediate family, and I was her Power of Attorney. I went to the hospital at least once every day, speaking to her doctor and nurses, and arranging for her care, until her death on Sunday afternoon February 6, 2011 at the age of 93. It was my responsibility to see to her needs during those last 23 days of her life. But I must commend Mary Spradlin and Gary Hughes who came many mornings and spent most of the day caring for Helen. Sheila and I would go in the evening and stay for several hours. Some nights we hired people with her money to stay with her through the night, while other nights we felt she was able to stay alone under the nurses' care. I knew she had desired that her entire family's life savings would go to the Coal Run Church of Christ. I discussed that with her just two days before she passed away, and indeed, that was her wishes. Helen had made me the Executor of her estate, and it took several months to get all of the estate settled, which included selling her car, selling her jewelry, selling her furniture, and clarifying her will in court. Finally, I had to sell her house, and it could not have pleased me more that Randy and Judy Looney, her wonderful next-door neighbors, were able to purchase the house. The final monetary gift to the church was about $1.5 million dollars. Many thanks to Sam Carter and Clarissa Friend who helped tremendously in getting the will probated and all legal work completed. None of us were compensated for our work in settling the Ratliff estate. We honored her specific wishes that "it all goes to the church." We were able to pay off the new church building in August 2011, and then remodel our old classrooms, and finish the new basement in order to start Kingdom Kids Preschool. Praise the Lord! Helen's parents, her brother, her husband and she had all agreed many years ago that they wanted their life savings to go to the Coal Run Church of Christ. And the last one living would see to that. Helen was faithful to carry out the wishes of her entire family. And the Coal Run Church of Christ was blessed to accomplish all of those building projects and become debt free largely because of the generosity and faith of that family, all of whom were members of our church.

I still believe God blessed our church in these amazing ways because we had been generous and faithful to help build many church buildings in Mexico for over 20 years, while we had not even painted the block exterior walls of our own building! Now we have one of the nicest church buildings in east Kentucky, with a large parking lot and drive through covered entrance!

2013 was a great year at Coal Run! We had 35 additions to the church and we launched the "Kingdom Kids Preschool." Clarissa Friend taught the 4-year-old class, and Terrie Carter the 3-year-old class. We had two grand-children attend the first year, Jay and Elijah. The preschool continues to be a great blessing to many children and their families!

A big help to me and blessing to our church was Aaron Davis. Aaron was raised in the East Point Church of Christ outside of Paintsville and started preaching some there when he was in college. He married Steve and Debbie Treap's daughter, Stephanie, who was raised in the Coal Run Church. He preached at Coal Run occasionally until he was hired as our Associate Minister in 2009. So, for a few years he typically preached at Coal Run one Sunday morning and two Sunday nights a month while continuing to serve at East Point part time as well. He also taught our high school class on Wednesday nights. Aaron is a dynamic preacher who has memorized much of the New Testament, as well as most of the sermons he prepares! We recommended Aaron be invited to speak at the Winter Worship and Workshop, hosted by Barnabas Ministries and he indeed preached an out-standing message. This opportunity launched Aaron's evangelistic ministry and what a ministry he is enjoying! Since then, he has preached in revivals and conferences across the brotherhood. In January of 2018 he was hired as the part time regular minister of his home church at East Point and has since baptized his dad, Danny, into Christ. His mother, Cheri, was a class-mate of ours at Kentucky Christian College back in the early 70's. East Point has grown and expanded their auditorium in recent years, for which we are grateful.

When Aaron left Coal Run and went to East Point, one of our deacons, Nathan Mills, who had been serving as our treasurer, volunteered to serve as our youth director. Nathan married Savannah, the daughter of Steve Slone, one of our elders. I was privileged to perform their destination wedding on Treasure Island Beach in June of 2009. That was the favorite wedding of my ministry. It was beautiful and very special! Several members of both families spent a week together in a nice resort, prior to the Friday evening sunset wedding on the beach. I think I was the only one in the wedding party wearing shoes! Nathan and Savannah have excelled in their careers. Nathan is the head of the Pharmacy Department and Savannah is the head of the Physical Therapy Department at Appalachian Regional Hospital in Prestonsburg. Their two daughters, Blakely and Jillian, are almost like my grandchildren. Nathan and Savannah along with Jon and Brittany Lyons are excellent leaders of the youth group. What a blessing they are to the Coal Run Church of Christ!

One of the most challenging baptisms we had at Coal Run was Linda Robinette. She was a friend of Angie Lane (a lady who has led several people to Christ) and was a resident of the nursing home in Pikeville for many years. Linda had been in a serious automobile accident which resulted in a surgery that left her bedfast and in chronic pain. Angie asked me to visit Linda, and she was quick to respond to the gospel call, but bed sores prevented her from being immersed in water. Linda was a very thoughtful and kind lady who had been mistreated by her husband and had endured a difficult life. I grew to love her and respect her faith and spirit, in spite of her pain and suffering. She went to wound care at Pikeville Medical Center many times for over a year before she healed enough to be baptized. I made arrangements with the nursing home and the chaplains at the hospital to use the hospital's modern baptistry, complete with a power lift body-sling. I was assisted by 2 chaplains, and nurses from the home in immersing Linda into Christ on April 1, 2015. Our elders and deacons were faithful to visit and serve her the Lord's Supper on Sundays and provide her with a tablet to watch our online services. Linda went to her heavenly home on September 8, 2020 having never been able to attend a church service in person; yet now she dwells in the house of the Lord forever!

During my ministry at Coal Run I was elected to serve as a Coal Run Village City Commissioner for 21 years. I enjoyed serving along-side of some wonderful people who helped our town to grow and prosper, including the wife of one of our elders, LaVerne Dye. She was an outstanding Mayor and now serves our church as a very efficient Treasurer.

My Mission Trips

Throughout the course of my located ministry, there were 21 times that I left my location and went to work for the Lord in a different place. All of these trips provided a blessing for me as well as for the people I went to help. Indeed, short term mission trips are a double blessing!

My first trip out of the country was to Saint George's, Grenada in March 1990. At that time my Dad was the Minister of the First Church of Christ in Eustis, Florida. He and David Elliott, a contractor and Eustis' elder, led this mission trip. I drove my family to Eustis, and then along with my Dad and Mom, and several other people from the Eustis church, we drove to Miami. There we met with other men from churches as far north as Ohio and flew to this island nation just north of Venezuela. The missionaries there had prepared a concrete slab and had gathered all the materials that were needed to begin construction the day after our arrival. We started the Jean Anglais Christian Church building on Monday morning, and on Friday afternoon we had the dedication of the building. It was complete with windows, doors, roof, pews, a stage and pulpit. We would work every day until 5 PM, then go to our seaside rental cottages, put on our swim trunks, go down the hill and swim in the Caribbean Sea for about 45 minutes. After a refreshing swim, we would go to the missionary's house for our evening meal. My mother helped other ladies prepare our meals. Thankfully, the people in Grenada speak English, though it is a different dialect than we are used to. This work trip was very well organized and productive, and I thoroughly enjoyed working with the men from Florida and Ohio to expand God's kingdom in that tropical paradise. At that time, I was still ministering to the Vansant Church of Christ, and members of the church gave me $755 for my trip, which was more than enough to meet all of my expenses. That was the only time that would happen! Through the years, the Coal Run church and individual members would help me with some of my expenses, for which I am very grateful, but they all involved a lot of my money as well.

My first of 18 mission trips to Mexico, was in February, 1992. Steve Treap organized this trip as well as most of the mission trips I took while serving at Coal Run. He always did a good job organizing our work and was good to work with. We flew to Harlingen, Texas, where missionary Clinton Looney lives, and then crossed the border to work on a children's home in Rio Bravo. There were twelve of us in all who made this trip, and the Mexicans called us the "twelve apostles." We slept on the concrete floor of the church building next to the children's home on air mattresses. We had one outhouse, and we had to build our own commode seat out of 2 x 4's. Steve Treap had told us to prepare to leave much of our clothing and some tools with the Mexicans, because they could use whatever we could give them. I think all of us did that, but while Steve was away from the church, the Mexican preacher, Thomas de la Cruz, was looking in Steve's bag of dirty clothes. In broken English, he asked me if he could take those clothes to a needy family. I said, "Yes, go on and take them." I soon found out that Steve had not gone through his clothes yet, and I had given away some of his work uniforms that he needed to keep. That is where I got the nickname, "Generous Jerry!" I was a little *too* generous with someone else's clothing! I felt bad and apologized, and Steve forgave me, but I never did that again. That trip really changed my attitude about my blessings in life. I had been rich all my life and didn't know it until I spent a week south of the border! There I saw poverty like I have never seen in our country. Yet in the midst of that poverty, most of the children were happy, well-groomed and nicely dressed, especially for school or church. It was always so good to go to Mexico with our brothers in Christ, because we always got a greater blessing than what we gave.

In February 1993, we again went with Clinton Looney across the border to Nuevo Laredo. The evangelists there were Jesus and his son, Rehu Menchaca. This time we had 19 men, most of whom slept in tents, and used one outhouse. I had intestinal issues one day but laid blocks the next, alongside of Buster Newsom, a retired brick mason and maintenance worker from our church. We were building a dormitory for Christian Mexican students to live in while they were enrolled in classes in the city. After church on Wednesday night, I was trying to say "good night" in Spanish to the folks leaving the service, but in my broken Spanish I was actually saying "good bottom" to the lovely Mexican ladies! One of the deacons told me of my mistake. I soon learned the Spanish word for "I'm sorry!" Years later we had a big group from Coal Run drive to Nuevo Laredo (including Sheila, our girls, my brother Jim and his son Joe) to work on three different projects in the area. It was a lot of driving and we never did that again!

In January 1994, we went with Jim Viers and crew to Salvatierra, Mexico, to work on a church building where Chon Avalos, and Dencil Duran of Mexican Evangelism Now were serving. (M.E.N. is now a part of Workers for Mexico, under the leadership of Francis Nash and Clinton Looney.). We flew to Leon, and then were transported on church vans to Salvatierra. This was the first of four trips that I made to this city of 35,000 people in central Mexico. I really love that city, church, and its members! The name of the city means "Land of the Savior." I have worked on the first and second floors of the church building, on the parsonage for the preacher, and on a church building outside of town in a community called Urireo. When we worked on the Urireo church building, both of my brothers were with me, and we all had the opportunity to preach at evening services. John, being fluent in Spanish, translated for Jim and me when we spoke. That was a special blessing that year. It was also at that church where we had a baptism, one Sunday evening, right after a very rare hailstorm. There was so much ice on the ground that the children made ice balls to play with. The baptism took place in a water cistern, with ice cold water! The preacher stood outside the cistern, while the shivering lady stood in the water waiting for him to stop his mini-sermon and baptize her into Christ!

There is a city about halfway between Leon and Salvatierra called Irapuato, where we also worked with Brother Jim Viers on a church building. In 2001 we worked on the church building in Leon with Hermilo Gasca, evangelist. On that trip were Sheila, both our daughters, and my brother Jim. We stayed downtown in Hotel Fundadores, where many stores and eateries are located. I still remember buying the best strawberry ice cream cones I ever ate next to the hotel for 30 cents each! We got a lot of good work done on the second story of the Leon Church of Christ and had a wonderful week!

I also had the opportunity to work in two different locations in Monterey. On one of those trips Rick Moore and I were roommates, staying in the home of Alex Valdez, brother of Alfredo Valdez, the preacher. That church is in a more prosperous part of the city called Guadalupe. Our work there involved putting a roof on the building, which was a little more dangerous than other projects we did south of the border. Through the years there were minor injuries from time to time, but God always protected us from serious injury or illness. We always had many godly Christians praying for us here in the states, and it was sometimes truly amazing how difficult situations were resolved while working for the advancement of God's kingdom in Mexico.

One other city I was blessed to work in four times was Saltillo. We flew to Monterey and then rode a bus or van through the desert mountains (beautiful scenery) about an hour and a half west to this very large city in northern Mexico. One of those times we worked outside of Saltillo at a community called Arteaga with evangelist Reynaldo Sanchez, working on their church building. The other three times we worked with Alfonso Olivares, on different buildings. One of the more unique trips involved Steve, Nathan Mills, Rick Moore, and me giving out reading glasses to poor people in four or five different locations around Saltillo. We developed a system where we had the people read different size fonts, and then we determined what type of glasses they needed. The glasses were provided by another mission, and we just helped in the distribution. They were all given freely to whoever came and needed glasses to help them read. We had many different kinds and allowed the people to choose their own glasses from different styles. We got to see many smiling faces that week, which in turn put a smile on our faces! I also enjoyed working with Francis Nash and Jaime Castro on a multi-purpose building for the Christian University in Queretaro. We had some good volleyball games after dinners on that trip. That University is doing a great job of training many young people in Mexico for Christian service!

The final work trip of my ministry at Coal Run was in January 2020. It was again with Steve, Rick, and Nathan. We went to Cancun to work on the second floor of a Church of Christ building in a poor section of town. We did take Friday to go swimming at a beach, but I think Florida has better beaches! I was 65 years old, and yet I was younger than Steve or Rick. We had to unload blocks from a truck to the second floor of the church building, where we mixed concrete and mortar, which we also had to put on the second floor. We also built castillos, which are like small metal cages for concrete pillars. Fortunately, we had a Mexican maestro to lay the blocks, and we were his helpers. I always managed to get in a long siesta after lunch, laying on the cool concrete lower floor of the building. My brothers were amazed that I could sleep so soundly on concrete, but it was no problem for me!

Two other mission trips I was blessed to take were with two other missions that our church supports. One was in 2006, working with International Disaster Emergency Services, building houses in Pearlington, Mississippi, a year after Hurricane Katrina had destroyed that community. IDES built a total of 39 houses for people who had lost basically everything. We stayed in a hotel in Slidell, Louisiana and drove over every morning to Pearlington to work. I actually worked on three different houses, doing everything from pouring concrete to hooking up a washer and dryer. We participated in the dedication of one house, where our brother from IDES presented a Bible and keys to the house to the happy recipient. The other trip was in the summer of 2007, when 33 members of the Coal Run Church of Christ went to Fort Thompson, South Dakota to work with Diamond Willow Ministries at the Crow Creek Sioux Reservation. We did a variety of things there, including working on a building, working on a playground, sorting and giving out clothes, and cleaning. Before arriving at Fort Thompson, many of us traveled in our own vehicles to Minneapolis, Minnesota and visited the Mall of America. On the way back, my car broke down at the Saint Louis Arch on Friday afternoon. Sheila and I had to have our car towed to a Ford dealership, rent a car, and get a hotel room, where we stayed until Monday evening when our car was repaired. We had to have the entire air-conditioning system replaced, and our church was kind enough to pay the expense of that repair--$1100! We did not get back home until Tuesday, and the delay caused me to miss the funeral services of two dear friends and mentors in ministry.... Mike Trent and Dick Damron. However, the highlight of that trip was the baptism of John Paul West in the Missouri River on Wednesday night, July 4, 2007. John Paul and his family are still faithful members of our church at Coal Run! God is good, all the time!

Three Natural Disasters

Over 44 years of ministry in the mountains, we encountered many problems with the weather. Usually it was snowstorms, power outages, and a lack of water. Sometimes it was too much water. In the 25 years we lived in the parsonage at Coal Run, the Levisa Fork of the Big Sandy River entered our basement three times. It was always 20 inches or less, but it certainly made a mess. Fortunately, the church always carried flood insurance which more than covered the damages to the parsonage, and we were able to make improvements on the basement each time a flood occurred. However, the worst flood of my lifetime was the 1977 flood.

At that time, we were living on Slate Creek outside of Grundy, Virginia, and ministering at Vansant. I actually was scheduled to begin my first revival meeting at the Garden Creek Church of Christ on the first Monday of April, when the main road in the town of Grundy was six feet under water. Obviously that revival had to be rescheduled! Though our apartment was not flooded, we did lose electricity and water for a few days. It was still cold outside, in fact, the day after the flood, it snowed. Fortunately, we were invited to go further up Slate Creek to the home of Sherman and Peggy Matney, members of the Grundy Church of Christ. Though they had no electricity, they did have a fireplace and a well behind their house where we could draw up water to drink. We stayed two or three days with them, along with Doug and Connie Matney, and George and Debbie Childress. Some delicious meat was cooked over an open fire, that would have thawed and ruined in their freezer. So, we ate heartily!

The main road between Grundy and Pikeville, US 460, had washed out in the flood. After three days, we learned that Pikeville had also flooded, including the parsonage where Sheila's parents lived. In fact, the river had gotten three feet in the upstairs of the parsonage and seven feet in the basement of the Coal Run Church building. E.W. actually took his fishing boat through the streets of Coal Run Village and rescued people from their houses. Sheila and I finally made it to Pikeville, going through Grundy, Vansant, Haysi, the Breaks and Elkhorn City. When we arrived in Coal Run, we found Mary and E.W. working, carrying everything out of the parsonage and cleaning the house. I stayed for two days helping them, and we slept in a classroom on the third floor of the Coal Run Church building. Sheila remained with her parents for several more days, but I went back to be at Vansant for Sunday morning service. The Vansant Church building had also flooded. Big Prater Creek got four feet in the basement of the building, so it was several weeks before we could resume Sunday school classes. I still remember taking apart an old upright piano with a hammer and using a wheelbarrow to get it out of the building. So many people and businesses suffered tremendous damage from that awful disaster! It was the result of eight inches of rain over a three-day period. And all of that was on top of a very cold and snowy winter in January and February of 1977. Because so many people had damage to their personal property or their places of employment, or were busy helping others whose homes had flooded, we had to be patient and wait for help on the church building. However, help finally came, and we fully recovered.

Another flood that was a very rare and unusual occurrence was the 2010 flood on Racoon Creek and Harless Creek in Pike County. It came on a Saturday in the middle of July. It started raining really hard in the afternoon with an unbelievably intense cloudburst. I remember unloading Hope food that Saturday night and all of us were soaked to the bone. We had no idea that at 9 PM, those two creeks had been turned into raging rivers, filling the valleys between the mountains with a deluge of water. One of our elders, Homer Edmonds, and his wife Naomi, lived on Raccoon Creek and had to hold on to each other walking from their house to the road through a very swift current up to their chest and neck in the dark! Four people died that night, but it could have been much worse. Several members of our church helped clean up different houses on Coon Creek in the days that followed. I personally helped at Homer's, Doug Hunt's, and Lee Burke's property. They were just three of many, many people who suffered the loss of so many possessions. It took weeks and weeks for the people to recover. International Disaster Emergency Services brought in a truck load of supplies, food, and water that went out from the Zebulon Church of Christ to help the suffering people. IDES also gave Zebulon around $22,000 that the church divided among 15 families. (Zebulon is the closest Church of Christ to Racoon Creek.) So, with the help of many good people, things eventually got back to normal.

One other quite unusual natural disaster occurred in March of 2012. Several tornadoes ripped through Eastern Kentucky, destroying homes and businesses in at least four counties. West Liberty and Salyersville took a direct hit. In fact, the West Liberty Christian Church where two of my uncles, my Dad, and one of my cousins had served as minister, had its' building totally destroyed! Thankfully, Pike County was spared, but Coal Run became a big part of helping the hurting. Once again, IDES came to our area and decided to build storage buildings to help hurting people who needed a place to store what possessions they had left. Over the next six months the floors, walls, and roofs of 51 storage buildings (8 x 12 feet) were prefabricated on the property of the Coal Run Church of Christ. The Pikeville Lowes provided building materials at a good discount to help with this project. In addition to IDES, many people donated money and time to buy the materials, build the buildings, and put them together in 51 different locations in four counties... Morgan, Magoffin, Martin, and Johnson. I was able to get information about where to put storage buildings in Morgan county from my cousin, Sallie Jo Nichols. It was good to reconnect with family in helping others in need. Buck Jones from our church was a huge help in this ministry, using his own truck and trailer to take out around 18 storage buildings, two at a time, and help put them up in those four counties. Steve Treap and the employees of his construction company helped tremendously with the prefabrication of the walls, floors, and roofs in our picnic shelter and then putting many together where needed. Many different men and women from Pike County Churches of Christ worked on this project. But we never would have been able to have completed 51 buildings without the help of the inmates of the Pike County Detention Center who came to our property on work release and worked for hours and days to get the buildings prefabricated. This was my mission project for 2012, as I worked about 40 days over five months on this project, working both on our property and in four different counties of East Kentucky. So out of all of my mission trips to many different locations, none were more demanding or time-consuming as what we were able to do in 2012. Thank God for the health and strength to help so many! The Coal Run church also gave $5000 to each of 4 different churches in East Kentucky to allow them to help their communities in their loss. God blesses us so that we can be a blessing!

Funny and Unusual Stories

In 1973, I was 19 years old and had just finished my first year at KCC. My future father-in-law, E.W. Damron, got me a preaching opportunity at the Shelby Church of Christ, a few miles south of Pikeville. I did not have a sermon to my name, and knew practically nothing about preparing a sermon... But I got a couple of sermon outline books and started. We had an elderly man by the name of Simon Sloan, who attended church every Sunday at Shelby. He was not a Christian, so one Saturday I went to visit him. I had Don Nash's notebook on basic principles to use in leading someone to Christ. I went through the first page with him on "God," and then this 82-year-old gentleman spoke up and said, "I have been thinking about being baptized." I laid my notebook down (never used it again), and thought, "Wow, this is easy." I asked him, "When would you like to be baptized?" He replied, "I don't know." I said, "Why not today?" He said, "Okay." We did not have a baptistry at Shelby, so we made arrangements to go to Coal Run to baptize him that afternoon in their baptistry. E.W. asked me if I needed any help. I said, "No, I know what to do." I got Mr. Sloan in the baptistry and said the right words and proceeded to try to lay him back into the water, but he did not want to go backwards. He was trying to go face forward. So, I knew I was in trouble. E.W. quickly got up and jumped across two choir pews, and across the front of the baptistry into the water, and said, "Give him to me!" He grabbed Simon by the head and pushed him backwards under the water. So, together, "we got 'r done!" That was my first baptism, and it wasn't as easy as I had assumed! This young preacher had a lot to learn.

My only failure at a baptism was in the mid-80s, when a young boy raised in the church desired to be baptized. He was afraid of water, however, because he nearly drowned in a pond near his home when he was very young. In fact, his cousin Mike Rife, pulled him out of the water and saved his life. When we got into the water, the boy said, "I've changed my mind, I've changed my mind," and out of the water he came. We asked him if he would be more comfortable if his dad was in the water with us to assist me. He said "yes." So, his dad changed clothes, and all three of us headed into the baptistry for a second try. But once again, he said he changed his mind and would not be baptized that day. Several years later Mike Rife, who had saved his *life* years before, and now the minister at Vansant, baptized him into Christ for the remission of sins to save his *soul*. This was Mike's first baptism at Vansant, and it's interesting to note that the young man was wearing a life jacket!

When I first began my ministry at Vansant, one Sunday after the morning service, Mike Rife's mother, Doris, said to me at the door, "Y'all go up!" I said, "Okay, we'll be there." I told my wife, Sheila, that we had been invited to the Rifes' for lunch. Sheila said, "That's odd, Doris didn't say anything to me about it. Just exactly what did she say?" I said, "Doris said, y'all go up!" Frustrated, Sheila said, "Jerry, she didn't mean it, that's just how they talk around here to be friendly." We went home and Sheila called Doris to tell her we weren't coming for lunch because I didn't understand what she meant.

Doris replied, "No, you all come on, I've already stopped at the store and got more food." So, we went up to the Rifes' and had a wonderful meal and an enjoyable time with Tobe, Doris, and their four children. But from that time on, Doris was careful how she greeted me at the door!

There is a small community near Coal Run across the river from the old Mullins school called "Broad Bottom." And at Grundy there is a small community across the creek from Mountain Mission School called "Long Bottom." One night at Vansant someone was put on the prayer list, and I said, "Yes, I think he lives at Broad Bottom." The people laughed and said, "You mean at Long Bottom!" Then I said, "Well, I know there is a *Broad Bottom* around here somewhere!" Then we all had a good laugh!

In the early 80s, a middle-aged couple started attending Sunday morning services at Vansant. They walked to church every Sunday morning with their little girl. I found out that they lived less than a mile from the church, but it was high up on a mountain at the mouth of Dry Fork Creek. I did not have a four-wheel-drive, so I parked at the foot of the mountain and began the climb. I walked to within 200 yards of their house and assumed I must be in the wrong place. "Surely no one lives up this narrow dirt road on the ridge of the mountain," I thought. I went back home and the next Sunday told them what I had done. They said, "You were on the right road, you just didn't go far enough." The next week, I walked all the way to their house and taught them the word of God. They did not have indoor plumbing, but they did have electricity. I soon baptized all three of them into Christ, and they faithfully attended every Sunday morning. I told our leaders that they would attend every service if we had a four-wheel-drive to pick them up. So, the church bought a repossessed Cherokee Chief from the bank for $2000, and we started bringing them to church every service. The mother was in her early 40s when she became pregnant with their second child. When the child was between 2 and 3 years old, he was still nursing his mother's milk. One Wednesday night, while I was teaching, the child decided to unbutton his mother's blouse and drink some warm milk. A sucking sound was soon heard throughout the auditorium, and I had to focus on the other side of the auditorium and try to keep a straight face while most of the congregation was sitting there with a big grin on their face. That night we all went home rejoicing that we had been in the house of the Lord! And that little boy grew up to be a fine young man, who served our country in the United States Marine Corps!

At Vansant, we usually had a different lady in the church take care of the communion trays each month. One service, on the last Sunday of the month, when the trays were uncovered for the Lord's supper, a strange aroma filled the room. The lady who was preparing the Lord's supper that month had been pouring the leftover grape juice back into the bottle each week. So, by the end of the month, the fruit of the vine had turned into fermented wine! It was not a miracle, but it was out of the ordinary! That Sunday, when we drank of the cup, a bitter, fizzing sensation filled our mouths. That was another day when the entire church went home rejoicing. We even had a big crowd back that night for a second helping! (Just kidding!)

While preaching at Vansant, I was the choir director, and we would have practice one hour before our Sunday evening service. We really enjoyed singing and had a pretty good choir... so it was a good experience. But one Sunday evening, one of our ladies asked the lady sitting next to her where she had been that morning and let her know she was missed. Boldly, the lady answered for all to hear, "Well, honey, I was over there at that cabin a rollin' in my sweet baby's arms!" What made it even funnier was the fact that she and her "sweet baby" were about 70 years old! That pretty well ended our choir practice for that evening. She later said that when her husband died, she would be "looking across the grave for her next man!" But I don't believe she ever remarried.

One Sunday I preached about the devil. I mentioned that the devil was present in our building and asked him to "please stand up." Of course, no one stood up, and I proceeded to preach about what I would do if I were the devil. It was a message about many of the things that are wrong in the church and in our world. The next morning at 6 AM, I got a phone call from a sweet widow in our church who was suffering from dementia. She said, "Mr. Bliffen, was that me you wanted to stand up in church yesterday?" At that point, I couldn't even remember what I had preached! I said, "What?"

She repeated her question, and I said "No, it wasn't you." Another Sunday I preached on tithing. At 6 AM the next morning the same dear lady called and asked me, "Who is that tithing around over there?" Again, I asked, "What?" She repeated her question, and I had to explain what tithing was, although I don't think she actually understood! But she was faithful to the Lord as long as she was able.

Another widow lady in our church lived right next door to the church. She had been a Pentecostal preacher before she was baptized at the Vansant church by a former minister. And she always wore a head covering when she came to church, as had been her practice in her former church. It was usually a scarf, but it was not that unusual for her to wear a shower cap to services. One time someone in the church bought her a bathroom rug set. However, she did not know what to do with the commode seat cover. So, one Sunday morning, here she came with a commode seat cover on top of her head -- lime green! I know I need a rug to cover my bald head, but if I ever get one, it will not be lime green! Once I went to visit her, and she asked me to pray for her "clot blood" that was on her wrist. She did have a knot on her wrist, so I prayed about it, and it soon went away. She then prayed a prayer of praise on Wednesday night, thanking the Lord for "that little preacher who came and healed me of my clot blood." One of the elders asked me after church if I had gone into the healing ministry!

One of the most unusual things that ever happened to me in an Officers' Meeting was when I was told by an elder at Vansant to visit every room in the Grundy Hospital and the Buchanan General Hospital, every day. Nobody in the world was doing that, and I was shocked that I was told to do it! Needless to say, I did not sleep well that night. That week I checked into the volunteer chaplaincy program at Buchanan General Hospital. It was an inter-denominational program, but I told the elders that I was willing to participate in it if they approved and they agreed. So, I joined that ministry, and eventually even became the director of the program. Nothing was ever again mentioned about me visiting every room in the hospital every day!

One of the funniest things that ever happened to me at Coal Run, was one Friday evening, a young man in the community, Tim Anders knocked on my door and asked to use the church's phone. He was living with his grandmother, a faithful and sweet member of our church, and he said she would not allow him to use her phone. Tim told me he had written a song for Michael Jackson and he had a toll-free number to reach him. Not wanting to bring him into my home where my wife and daughters were because he was a drug addict, I took him across the parking lot to my church office and allowed him to use the phone. I had no idea what he might do next. He indeed called a toll-free number for a large hotel chain in Chicago and asked to speak with Michael Jackson. The lady he spoke to must have asked him, "and who should I say is calling for him?" And Tim thought for a moment, "I can't say Tim Anders... That won't get me anywhere." He then thoughtfully and boldly replied, "Timotheus Andreus!" I had the biggest smile on my face... I wish you could have been there! In the meantime, Sheila had called our neighbor and elder, Homer Edmonds, to go to the church and check on the situation. He soon came to the office and said, "Tim, you get out of here, you can't tie up the church's phone." I guess that is one song Michael never got to record. However, years later telling that story to one of our deacons, he replied, "Maybe that's where Michael Jackson got the song 'Beat It.' Homer told Timotheus to beat it!"

I know some of these stories are hard to believe, but they are true. I am not creative enough to make this stuff up. In dealing with people through the years I have learned that people are like eggs -- some are "cracked," some are "hard-boiled," some are "deviled," some are "scrambled," and some are "fried." But as followers of Jesus, we love them all!

Sheila and I retired in July of 2020 at age 66, after 44 years of full-time ministry. Kentucky Christian University honored us with the President's Award, and the church at Coal Run presented us with many gifts. My retirement thus far has been the 5 "G" program...God, Grandchildren, Golf, Garden, and Grass (the kind you mow!) The past year Sheila and I have been blessed to enjoy traveling to Florida and several other places. I have thoroughly enjoyed preaching in several sister congregations since retirement, and Sheila and I treasure the many Christian friends we have made in these churches. God's people are the best people on earth and we look forward to an eternity with all of them. God has certainly blessed us with many wonderful years of Christian service and we plan to continue serving Him as long as we are able. I'm so thankful for the very talented and dedicated man God sent to step in and lead the church at Coal Run into the future ... Brother Trey Mouton. God truly answers prayer!

Jim Bliffen family
Jim, Joe, Joni, Jacki, Jeremy

Chapter 13

My Brother, James Daniel (Jim) and Joni Bliffen

by Jim Bliffen

I began my ministry my senior year at Kentucky Christian College in 1976. I had just finished soccer practice and was in the shower when my cousin, Tom Thomas, came into the shower room and said, "Hey cuz, you want to sing in a quartet?" I said, "Sure, why not." I didn't think I could sing in any group and had never sung in public for anyone [unless forced]. But I had made a vow to God back when I was just a freshman that if anyone asked me to do something for the Lord, I would at least try. In a moment of unguarded weakness, I agreed to be in the quartet. I thought it would just be a joke.

I ended up singing tenor in the quartet "Tribute." I did not believe that it would ever amount to anything, but I was wrong. We ended up singing for churches and camps all over the country. We traveled as far west as Dodge City, Kansas, and as far east as New York City. We traveled as far South as Florida, and as far North as Indiana. We sang in hundreds of Churches and dozens of camps. At the height of our popularity, we had to begin limiting our engagements to just three a month. Though we started singing at KCC, my father recruited all the other members of our group, Tom Thomas, Stuart Shepherd, and Tim Stapleton to become students at Mid-South Christian College in Senatobia, Mississippi. I had been invited to sing with another group called the Advocates in New York, but when the other guys decided to go to Mississippi, I went with them and became a student recruiter for Mid-South Christian College.

In 1978, we began travelling throughout the Mid-South area singing in Churches and camps. We bought our own van, sound system, and paid for all our expenses without ever asking for money. We just accepted whatever a church or camp offered us and love offerings. At a camp in Monticello, Arkansas, the first summer we traveled, I met my future wife, Joni Smith. I was already a college graduate and had actually spent an extra year in college gaining college credit toward a Bachelor of Theology, but I was mainly there to play soccer and sing in the group (I never got the B.Th. degree). Joni had just finished her Junior year in High School, and her parents had made her go to camp that year. Joni lived in Hot Springs, Arkansas and we saw her and the youth group she was a part of several times over the next year. If we were singing in Arkansas [which we often did] she was there with her family or her youth group. We were invited to sing in Hot Springs several times, and we always went because her family really supported us.

At the time I thought Joni was too young for me. We always had girls at camps and churches that flirted with us, but I never took any of them seriously. Joni was different. She was bright, clever, beautiful, and persistent. She captured my heart with several clever letters she wrote me. I did not respond in kind. She actually sent me a letter with multiple choice answers so that all I had to do was check the appropriate box and send it back. I answered that one. But at one point she almost broke up with me because she hadn't heard from me for a month or two. She forgave me and came to Mid-South Christian College as a student in 1979. The group continued to travel, but we had new personnel. Tim left the group to marry Daphne McGuire who played piano for us over the summer of 1978. Stuart left the group to go back to Kentucky Christian College. My brother John joined the group and Terry Anderson became our piano player. We continued to travel for two more years. Then Tom and Terry left, so John and I continued to travel with Becky Bliffen playing the piano, and Jim McQuarry playing the guitar. I had a few offers to sing with other groups, but Joni and I were engaged to get married, and I did not want that kind of life [traveling all the time] to interfere in our relationship. I then began to search for a located pulpit ministry.

I applied at First Christian Church of Demopolis, Alabama to become their minister. They hired us with 100% of the vote. We had nearly nine years of fruitful ministry in Demopolis from 1981-1989. We still have many very good friends there. Later in my ministry, the Demopolis Church became one of our best supporters as we went to the mission field. This was a former Disciples of Christ Church. They had left the denomination when a Disciples minister, who had been trained at Johnson Bible College, led them out of the denomination. However, they still had a lot of close relationships with the denominational churches around them and insisted that I join the local Ministerial association. Our church actually joined with the Presbyterian and Episcopal churches for softball and Vacation Bible School. We continued to join these churches for a while because we didn't have enough people for a softball team, and they were using Standard Publishing VBS material. But as the Church began to grow, we began to break those relationships and held our own VBS and had our own softball team.

As a part of my association with the Ministerial Association, I became a part of a quartet. It was started to sing at a community Thanksgiving service. It was composed of me and two other Baptist ministers. We could not find anyone in the Association to sing bass, so we got a fellow from the choir of one of the other members to sing with us. It was supposed to be a one-time thing, but soon churches started asking us to come and sing for them at revivals and special meetings. Before long we were singing for store openings and community events. I told Joni that we sang in all the best parking lots in town! The group was called "Jim and the Baptists" because I was the only non-Baptist in the group. The name came when people would ask where I was and they said, "He's out singing with the Baptists." The other guys would say I was the only Christian in the group because I was from the First Christian Church. I really had a great relationship with those guys and had a lot of fun times singing with that group. Singing with those guys was never a chore. We got together at 6:00AM on Tuesdays and Thursdays to play Racquetball and practice music from 7-8AM and then we would go to work. Those kinds of relationships with leaders from denominational churches were a big help to me when I got to Papua New Guinea as a missionary much later in life.

Our two children, Jacki and Joe, were born in Demopolis. We loved the people in the town, but we did not want to raise our children in the atmosphere of racial prejudice. We left Demopolis after nine years of ministry and moved to Montgomery, Alabama in 1989 where we served for three years with the Southeast Christian Church. There we struggled a bit as we felt like the church was in constant turmoil. But we made some really good friends there, who are still friends to this day. One of those friends, a gentleman named Greg Hopkins, would play a major role in a later decision. I met Greg at a men's retreat in Alabama. Some of us preachers were playing Bible Trivia. Greg and some of his laymen friends were playing the same game at the next table. We decided to play against each other. Us preachers thought that would we defeat these laymen for sure until we asked the question, "Can you give the Hebrew names for Shadrach, Meshach, and Abednego?" Greg knew the answer! We gave up.

From Montgomery we moved to Wauchula, Florida in January of 1992. The church in Wauchula had seven ministers in the previous nine years. We decided that even if we got fired there, it would not reflect badly on my resume since they had the reputation of being preacher eaters. We wanted to go to Florida to get closer to our family and we enjoyed being closer to Mom and Dad, Bob and Jane. The people there were mainly involved with agriculture. I got into trouble during one Bible study I held with the Senior Citizen group when I discussed agriculture. I was teaching concerning Jesus' story about a fig tree that failed to produce. I talked about a small orange tree a person in our church gave to me and its lack of production. I said I had planted it in full sun, watered it, and looked for it to produce oranges. But after a few years it only produced one orange. So, I fertilized it, got rid of all the weeds around it, and gave it its own sprinkler head to water it. I then explained that if it did not produce after that I would get rid of the tree. I was trying to make the same point Jesus was making, that we need to produce fruit for the kingdom in our life, and that if we are not being productive for the Kingdom, Jesus is aware and will not tolerate it, because He has provided us with all we need to produce fruit in our life. Suddenly a hand went up in the back of the class. "Preacher, what kind of fertilizer did you use?" I said that I couldn't remember, but it was some kind of fertilizer that I got from Walmart. I tried to explain that it didn't matter because the point was the plant needed to produce like we all need to be productive. Another hand went up. "Preacher, you should be getting your fertilizer from the Davis family, not that cheap stuff from Walmart." That began a rather lengthy conversation concerning the type, brand, amount, and efficacy of fertilizer. All the while I continued to try to explain the main point, that we all need to produce fruit for the kingdom. However, they were no longer interested in the Bible study as their attention was fully fixed on my orange tree. There was a very lengthy discussion as to what kind of tree it was, how much fruit it should produce, what was my soil composition, and on, and on, and on. Though I tried as hard as I could, I could never bring the conversation back to the story of Jesus. I finally gave up and called on one of the members to dismiss us with a word of prayer. I never discussed agriculture in that Bible study group again!

A significant spiritual event occurred one night just before we left the ministry in Wauchula. My pharmacist, Miles Judah, caught me in choir practice one Wednesday night and asked, "What are you doing after choir practice?" I said I was going home and going to bed. He said, "No. You're coming with me!" Miles explained that he was prescribing medicine for a man who had cancer, and that he knew because of the kind of medicine and the amounts that the doctors were giving him, that he was about to die. Miles explained that this man, named John, was a well-known scoundrel and that if he died in his present spiritual condition, he was going to Hell. Miles said that the Lord had laid it on his heart to go talk to this man. He told me that he was going to do all the talking and that he was just taking me along in case he made a mistake. When we got to John's house that night, Miles immediately got a phone call as we entered the house. He went in another room to deal with the call and I sat alone with John, who I had never met, and began a conversation with him. We talked about the weather, college football, and other inconsequential topics until Miles returned to the room. Miles immediately took over the conversation with, "John, we didn't come here to talk to you tonight about the weather, football, or any of that stuff. We came to talk to you about your soul." Both John and I were stunned by Miles' blunt statement. But Miles continued by telling him that he knew John was very sick and was going to die. He told him his only hope was in Jesus Christ. We continued talking to John for over an hour. John's biggest problem was he didn't think he could be forgiven for all his sins. He even said, "But Miles, you don't know what I've done!" Miles said, "John, this is Wauchula, everyone knows what you've done." We went on to explain that God can forgive any sin and any sinner. I remember telling him the story of David and his sin and that God had forgiven him. Finally, John said, "You mean He can forgive even me?" We said yes. That if he would believe that Jesus is God's Son, call out to God, confess that he was a sinner and turn to God, and be baptized, God would wash away his sin. John said, "I do believe in Jesus and want Him to save me." We asked when he would like to be baptized and he said, "Right now." We prayed and took John to the church to be baptized the same hour of the night. When I was baptizing John, I was a little frightened. His cancer had left him skin and bones. His body felt frail as I lowered him under the water. When I brought him back from his watery grave, I asked John if he was alright? John said, "Alright? I have never felt better in my life." John went to be with the Lord less than a week later. After that, I always kept in mind when I was going to speak to a person about their soul that I wasn't there to talk about the weather, football, or other inconsequential topics. That would make a big difference in my ministry going forward.

After eight years of ministry in Wauchula, I received a phone call from Greg Hopkins. Greg had moved from Montgomery to Huntsville, Alabama. He told me the Huntsville Christian Church was looking for a new minister and wondered if I would be interested in coming back to Alabama. I told him that I wasn't really interested in Alabama as a state, but I did see potential in Huntsville. It took about a year, but after a long time of interviewing and miscues and difficulties, Huntsville finally decided they were interested in me and hired me. We moved back to Alabama July 4, 1999. Huntsville was a great ministry for us for a long while. The church grew steadily and doubled in size in five years. Many people were won to the Lord and I baptized more people in that five years than in all my other ministries put together. We moved to multiple worship services, changed from committees to a leadership ministry system, enlarged the building and parking lot, added a preschool, started several new ministries designed to reach our community, and added new staff. After serving in Huntsville for eleven years and hiring several new staff members, there were some difficulties in our ministry. We decided that it would be best if we found a new ministry. This was a very difficult decision for us. We still feel like Huntsville is home for us and we still have many dear friends there.

We moved to Durant, Oklahoma in 2010. The church was a new church that had just separated from the Disciples of Christ over their acceptance of homosexuality. The people that interviewed me told me that they wanted to be a strong Independent Christian Church and they needed someone who was strong in that church to lead them. I had served in a former Disciples Church and I thought I could be the one to help lead them to become what they said they wanted to be. I felt that this would be our final located ministry and that we would be in Durant until we retired.

After serving there for a year, Joni went on a mission trip to Cambodia. After she came back, we were out walking in our neighborhood when she asked me if I thought I could ever become an overseas missionary. I thought she had lost her mind. We were just into our second year of a ministry where I had promised the people I would stay until I retired or died. We had just bought a house, and we were living closer to her family than we ever had. But I answered as spiritually as I knew how. I said, "I don't think God has called me to do that." Joni said she thought God was calling her. I explained that we were a team, we had always been a team, and that God would not call her to something He did not also call me to. I thought this notion would be temporary, but Joni decided to pray that if God was calling her, He would call me too.

That answer came a just a year later. As we continued to minister in Durant, we were being drawn closer to the mission field and Pioneer Bible Translators. We received a newsletter in the mail from Johnson University that told of a new online program they were starting in Intercultural Studies. They said a person could get their degree from home and not have to attend classes on the campus in Knoxville. Joni and I got married before she finished college so she wanted to go back and get her degree. I agreed that she should enroll. Joni was the first student to sign up for the online Intercultural Studies program. She noticed that many of the professors were from Pioneer Bible Translators. Around that time, we had a visitor named Marsha Miles who is a longtime friend of Joni's family. She also had been a member of Joni's youth group many years ago. Marsha had been a translator working with PBT for over 30 years. I didn't know at the time she came to visit us that she had spoken to Joni's youth group nearly 40 years earlier, and Joni had decided she also wanted to be a missionary. I had some missionaries in my family, and I knew the kind of struggles they faced in their ministry. I had no desire for that kind of life. Nevertheless, Marsha invited us to come and have a look at the new PBT offices in Dallas, Texas just 2 hours away.

When we went and visited the offices, everyone there kept telling us that they had been praying for a couple like us to come join the team. I remained unconvinced that this was what we needed to do, but I was open to the idea of coming back to PBT for a program they have every year called Discovery. We could only come for a day. At the end of that day, Marsha introduced us to some people from Papua New Guinea. I was talking to the branch director at that time while Joni was speaking with another person named William Butler. William had lived in PNG for over 30 years translating the Waran New Testament. He was very sick and in a wheelchair. He told Joni that he had been taken off his translation ministry because the accountant for the branch had died very unexpectantly. He was the only one in the branch that knew anything about finances, so he had to assume her duties. He spent five years working in the finance office but had to come home when he had gotten very ill. He explained to Joni that he was afraid he was going to die, and that the New Testament translation would never be completed unless the Lord sent an accountant to take his place. When Joni relayed his story to me, the Lord spoke to my heart and said, "Get ready, you're going to Papua New Guinea." William told us later that he was really sick that day and had decided not to go to Discovery that night, but he felt like the Lord was telling him he needed to go. So, he came, not realizing what the Lord was calling him to do.

We both had to attend classes at Johnson University online to prepare us for intercultural ministry. Eventually Joni earned her bachelor's degree, and I received my master's degree, both in Intercultural Studies. We raised the needed funds and completed our training after a year of hard work. In January 2014 we left the USA for PNG. We served two terms as PBT missionaries in PNG. Joni served as the Administrator of Finance and I worked in the area of Scripture Impact and Church Relations.

When we first arrived in PNG, we had to attend a twelve-week jungle survival class called the Pacific Orientation Course, or POC. There were twelve couples there, mostly younger people than Joni and me but there were a few older people there also. I was the oldest man in the group at the age of 59. POC was a rustic setting which left many of the other students complaining about the austere conditions. Joni and I thought of it as a rustic church camp. We had spent a lot of time in those over the years. A big difference was the fact that our showers were bucket showers, and our water heater was a wood burning stove. Each member of the course took turns getting up early, collecting the wood, and lighting the fire. We also had to take shifts working in the cafeteria.

We spent the first six weeks being trained on how to survive in the bush. We spent the next five weeks with a family in the village of Kumal. We were given Tok Pisin language lessons, lessons on culture, and practical lessons such as cooking and baking over a fire. As part of our training, we also had to swim a mile and learn to walk on the bush trails high in the mountains during rainy season. We hiked every Monday, Wednesday, and Friday. On Tuesday and Thursdays, we went swimming trying to get in good enough shape to swim a mile. By the end of our time in the camp we both had swam our mile in the hour they allotted for us to complete the task. There was also a long hike to a neighboring mountain that we had to modify because of a terrible hiking day for both Joni and me.

For me it began at lunch. They were serving what they called PNG kaikai or Papua New Guinea local food. That was the day I found out that I cannot eat kaukau, a type of potato, that is a staple food of the local people. I began vomiting immediately after lunch was over. We had a one-hour rest period before our hike that day and I was feeling much better by the time we left on our hike, but I did not eat again. The hike we were to take was to be the longest one yet. POC was located at the top of a high mountain. We hiked down to the base of the mountain on the road and then we were to return up to the top of the mountain on bush trails. Joni started getting hot and tired on the way down the mountain. I felt fine when we started up but before long, we were both in trouble. Joni had not brought enough water along and had finished her water by the time we reached the bottom of the mountain. She then began finishing off my water too. I was fine when we reached the bottom but by the time we started back up, I was getting in trouble too. We were exhausted very quickly. Our athletic director, Russ, was with us and he continued to encourage us as we trudged along. He quoted the entire book of Ephesians and part of the book of Philippians to us as we moved along. Sometimes we would only take four or five steps and then we would have to stop and rest. It was starting to get dark and malaria car-rying mosquitos were constantly hovering around us in the rainforest bush. Finally, after several hours, we reached a small village that had a road. The rest of our hiking team were waiting for us at that village. POC sent a tractor and trailer after us to get us the rest of the way back up the mountain. I had some major cramps that night.

When we had completed our class work, we went to the village of Kumal to spend the next five weeks. The family that took care of us there was called our "Was family" or "watch family." They became very dear friends for the next seven years. Joni still talks to them occasionally from here in the states. Our house there had no electricity or plumbing. They made us an outhouse that was the envy of all our POC friends because it had a wooden toilet seat. They made us a shower room complete with our own old oil drum to store our washing water. There was often a film on top of our water, but it was refreshing, no hot water. Our house had rotten boards in it and Joni broke through the floor one day. We found out that the metal roof was not fastened down at all when the wind from a large storm blew the metal around and water poured in on our bed. We moved our bed and put a pot under the water coming in. The next day our family went up on the roof and moved the metal around to cover the hole. Joni said the thing she missed the most was ice. I missed Coke. I lost 30 pounds over my POC experience.

Our training came in very handy as we began our ministry in PNG. I had many trips to the bush. One of those trips was to a bush Church of Christ Bible College called Gandep. I made five trips to this campus. Our trip usually consisted of a car ride for several hours, a boat ride for several more hours, and a hike for three to five hours. On one trip I was traveling with my good friend and fellow expat missionary, Kevin. After about the first hour of the trip we came to a bridge. Usually, we crossed the bridge with little problems, but we did have to watch out for rotten boards. This time we saw smoke rising into the air as we approached the bridge. Someone had burned it a short time before we got there. All that remained was the metal frame, the frame of a flatbed truck, and some heavy logs that had supported the bridge. We crossed over walking on the metal. When I reached the other side, I attempted to step over a very large log that was still burning. The log was very high, and my short legs did not allow my feet to get all the way to the top of the log. I stepped up close to the top, but the burned bark broke under my boot. I lost my balance and fell into the smoldering ashes. I soon realized that the ashes were burning my face. What really distressed me was what the Gandep students did to help me. They immediately ran down to the creek dipped a rag in the water and came back to wash the ashes off my face. The last thing I wanted was that water in an open burn. The burns were small, and they healed fine. When we returned, we had a new leader. He was really incredulous that the first guide had led us white skin missionaries over a burning bridge. Instead, he led us around the bridge to the creek, which we stepped over with no problem, and then returned to the trail.

We found out after we were there for a short amount of time that we arrived in PNG at a very special time. PBT had been in PNG for 40 years and many of the translations that had been started years ago were completing. We got to attend three dedications, the Tay, Mbore, and the Waran. They were all great, however the most important one to Joni and I was the Waran New Testament dedication. This was the people group that William Butler was working with. We had come to PNG to free William from the finance office so he could complete his translation work. In June 2019, the Waran people dedicated the New Testament.

Joni and I boarded a plane in Madang and flew an hour to Likan village. We then boarded a motor canoe (a dugout log canoe with an outboard motor on the back) and traveled three hours to the village of Yar where the dedication was held. The people greeted us with in their traditional celebratory manor, by splashing water all over us, soaking us. People were everywhere singing and dancing. We helped with meals and celebrated with the people. One of the main groups leading in the celebration was a very good bamboo band. They had stacks of different sized bamboo and they beat the hollow tubes with their rubber sandals. They played all night long right outside the house where Joni and I were trying to sleep as they prepared for the dedication celebration the next day. They played the same tune over and over again. Occasionally the music would stop for few moments only to gain momentum a short while later. Joni was getting irritated by the constant tune and about three in the morning she threatened to go burn their bamboo. She said, "They keep playing the same song over and over again!" I said, "But they are singing different words!" We were both right. We found out the next day that the song they were singing was about the Word of God coming to the Waran people and the difference it was making and was going to make in their lives. They knew that there would be people from 14 or 15 language groups that lived around them, so they learned the song in all those languages so their visitors could hear the message about the Gospel in their own heart language. The bamboo band about drove us crazy, but we were glad we didn't burn their instruments. Those Bibles have now been vastly distributed among the Waran people.

During our first term, I joined the Ministers Fraternal in Madang and began to form relationships with many of the ministers in town. I often spoke in their churches and held Bible studies with our national translators. I also took charge of a Sunday night program called Sing and Share that was mainly for the missionaries in town. We met for prayer, a time of sharing our concerns, and communion. Several missionaries from other translation agencies working in town also met with us.

One of my most unusual relationships was with Father Hunter, the Anglican minister in town. He was one of the main leaders in the Ministers Fraternal. He was often frustrated with the lack of action by the ministers in town and often turned to me to get things done. He was an Australian who had grown up in PNG. He invited me to come and speak at his church one Sunday morning. I knew it was a very formal church, so I wore my formal church missionary clothes. I wore dark pants, a white shirt, and tie. I knew that I would sweat because the church would be 98 degrees, so I also put on an undershirt so that I would not sweat through my white shirt and have it stick to me. When I got there, he took me into a back room where he had me put on a robe on top of all of that. I sweated through my undershirt, my white shirt, and the robe. You could have rung the sweat out of it all. Later, he had me come preach again and I just wore a shirt that time. During the service he asked if I wanted to help with communion. I reminded him that I was not an Anglican and I didn't know how they did communion. He said I should just follow them. If they kneeled, I should kneel. If they raised their hands, I should raise my hands. The best part was that I would get the first drink from the one cup they used for communion. Given the amount of Tuberculosis and other diseases common in the country, that seemed like a good idea to me. So, I agreed to participate. Of course, they use real wine, which was quite a shock to my nonalcoholic palate. All I could think was how in the world did I get here, preaching in an Anglican Church, serving Anglican communion, and living across the street from it all 8,000 miles from home in Papua New Guinea.

I also took many trips to the bush to teach in Bible colleges, to do literacy surveys, to preach in the churches, and to help in setting up the groundwork for a new multilingual translation project called the Lower Ramu Project. During our second term Joni was elected to become the Director of Support Services. All of our missionary partners who worked in the area of maintenance had left the country, so Joni asked me to help with that work, too. I spent a good amount of time working with our PNG national workers. By this time, my health was not good enough to travel to the bush very often so most of our time was spent in Madang, the PNG town where we lived.

Our third term In PNG didn't go very well. It began with a car accident involving us and a security company vehicle. It was my fault, so I agreed to pay for the damages. Not long after that I injured my back. I could not walk straight up without a cane. It took a few weeks to recover from the pain. We knew our time in PNG was close to being finished. We announced at the branch Annual General Meeting that we were only going to stay for one more year and then leave for the states in the summer of 2021. Joni and I took a weekend in a local resort to celebrate her birthday and get away from the stress of having to deal with problems, and the stress of having to deal with our Annual General Meeting. It was at this time the Lord began to reveal to Joni that we would not be in PNG as long as we thought we would.

A couple of weeks later I was bitten by a dog that we were watching while one of the members of the branch was away on vacation. The dog bit my hand and then savagely attacked one of the other missionaries that was trying to help get the dog under control. He ended up getting a large number of stiches in both arms. I only had one bite on my hand, so the doctor looked at it, cleaned it with betadine, and bandaged it. I thought I was healing when cellulitis formed in my hand and began moving down my arm. After a few days it also broke out on my knee which had not been injured. I went to see the doctor and he prescribed a series of antibiotic shots, one a day for seven days. I had to stay home and keep my hand elevated. I finished the treatment with more antibiotics taken by mouth after the shots. I knew my great-grandfather had died because of a cat scratch that developed into cellulitis, so I followed the doctor's instructions closely and made a full recovery.

Soon after that, we were hearing in PNG that the COVID-19 virus was spreading throughout the world, and many countries were beginning to close their borders. We had a leadership meeting where we discussed what could happen in PNG if the worst-case scenarios occurred. The main problem we feared was that Australia would close their borders, cutting us off from emergency health care. It was at this meeting that Joni and I decided we needed to get out of PNG as fast as we could, or we would be separated from any doctors that could help us if we became seriously ill. At that time, we thought we may be in the states for as long as 6 or 7 months. We bought our tickets and began packing up our apartment and offices. On the day before we left, we heard that Australia, the country we were flying into in order to get a connection back to America, was closing its borders at 9:00PM, on the day we were flying out of PNG, our plane was supposed to land in Sydney, Australia at 9:30PM. We decided to leave Madang and fly to Port Moresby, the capital of PNG and the only international airport in the country and see what happened. We flew to Port Moresby, but we were not allowed to board our plane to Australia. Australia had already closed their borders at 10:00AM. There were several others trying to get to Australia, but all of us were stuck right there in Port Moresby. Finally, after several tense hours, the officials in PNG were able to get special permission for all of us to board the plane. We were literally the last people that were allowed to fly into Australia who were not Australian citizens.

We returned to the states on March 23, 2020. We have been unable to return, but plan to do so in the near future, for a few months. Since the time we left, the branch in PNG has suffered the loss of one of our teammates, and two of our teammates as well as three of our national workers have tested positive for Covid19. Our teammates there are under incredible stress. We are planning to return so that the few missionaries who have been stranded in PNG can leave for a while and get out of the country to have a vacation. After they return to PNG, we plan to leave the country and return to the states permanently.

We will continue to serve with PBT here in the states. Upon our return to the states, Joni will assume the job of an international accountant and I will join the Development Team. Though we will not be overseas, our influence will grow to international levels instead of being restricted to PNG. We will continue to live in northwest Arkansas helping to care for Joni's parents. Of course, all of this is dependent on the Lord's will. One thing this past seven years has taught me is to hold my plans loosely and wait to see what the Lord has in mind.

John D. Bliffen family
Elizabeth Ann, Carol Marie, Becky, John, John Thomas

Chapter 14

MY BROTHER, JOHN DEAN
AND BECKY BLIFFEN
BY JOHN D. BLIFFEN

O n September 21, 1979, my father told me, "Today, you have become a man, my son." It was the day I got married to Rebecca Regis Bliffen. I graduated from Mid-South Christian College with a Bachelor of Arts in Christian Ministry in 1981. The same year I became the Minister of Senatobia (Mississippi) Christian Church. In 1983, we moved to Cincinnati to attend graduate school at Cincinnati Christian University. There we hosted the first international services office for *Team Expansion* in our living room at 941 Grand Ave. In the summer of 1984, we went on a mission internship to Uruguay. We returned to Mid-South Christian College from 1984 to 1985 and, in 1985, I graduated from CCU with a MA in Theology. Then I became Minister of Missions with the *Wilmington (Ohio)* Church of Christ from 1986 to 2009.

We went to language school in Costa Rica in 1986 where our oldest daughter Carol Marie was born. We went full time with Team Expansion to Uruguay in 1987. We worked in a church planting team in Uruguay through 1995. There the team established 5 small congregations which eventually merged into Iglesia Cristiana Montevideo which continues today and has now grown to have various ministries in Uruguay and missions in Brazil and Argentina. John Thomas was born in Uruguay in 1988. Elizabeth Ann was born in Wilmington, Ohio (while on furlough) in 1990. All three of our children have gone to various Bible colleges and are seeking to serve the Lord in whatever way he leads them.

We moved to Miami, Florida as a team in 1996 to plant a Hispanic church in Miami, known as *Iglesia Cristiana en West Kendall*. This church later merged with the bilingual South Winds Christian Church on Quail Roost Drive in Miami. Living in Miami we also did outreach in Cuba and Ecuador. Our work in Cuba in cooperation with White Fields Evangelism and POEM resulted in 40 house churches throughout the whole country of Cuba in the first 20 years of existence. The Cuba Bible Institute was formed in 2005 and continues to train Cuban evangelists to this day who serve this growing house church movement. The *Iglesia Cristiana en Cotacachi*, Ecuador was formed in 2003 from a member of our church from Miami.

In 2009 we moved from Miami to Memphis, Tennessee to become Director of Church Relations at *Mid-South Christian College*. We continued training Hispanic church leaders and others there at MSCC. In 2012 we started *Iglesia Cristiana en East Win*, which continues to this day under the leadership of one of our graduates from MSCC.

From January 2017 – December 2019 we lived in Granada Spain helping to establish the Team Expansion team there. Much of our work was in structuring the missionary team and helping launch a media ministry. During the last year (2020) over 30 Bible study groups have started through the training of the team there in Granada.

From January 2020 we have returned to Memphis to continue work with Mid-South Christian College. We continue to train Hispanic church leaders and others. We also began *Mid-South Hispanic Ministry* which works to start more Hispanic Christian churches in Arkansas (in partnership with *Arkansas Church Planting Network*) and in West Tennessee and North Mississippi. One new Hispanic church began in Little Rock, AR in January 2021 (Comunidad Cristiana, Little Rock) and other church planters are being recruited and planned for two other future Hispanic church plants in coming years.

Bible College Years

Larry Griffin and I had attended college together at Mid-South Christian College, which at that time was located outside of Senatobia, Mississippi. While we were both in college, we represented two groups of students which had friendly debates about whether preaching or missions was more important. Larry was convinced that missions was the most important way to fulfill God's commands. I represented those who were content to stay behind and preach in US churches. Sometimes I felt that Larry took some things to extremes. There was the time that we had a mission's emphasis for our Thanksgiving dinner, where we were to have rice and bread and water to help us see the needs of the rest of the world. It would have been okay, but for some reason the rice got burned, so it was only bread and water, and some students didn't feel very thankful.

My friend Larry was recruited by Doug Lucas to go to Uruguay in 1982 with the first Team Expansion team. On Doug's first recruiting visit to our campus, he had an interesting experience. The college was located on 160 acres out in rural Mississippi. From the nearest town you drove 10 miles west on the main road, and then two miles out into the wilderness. In preparation for a campus recruitment visit, Doug arrived late one night. Out of the darkness a young man appeared with an arrow in one hand while holding a possum by the tail in the other hand. Ray was wearing shorts and no shirt. I guess Doug thought that he was already in jungles on a mission trip. Later that night Doug went to the bathroom and saw the possum hanging in the shower having been skinned and cleaned! Ray, the possum slayer, was known to have some eccentric ways, like making popcorn with motor oil. Well, he found a slow cooker and cooked that possum in my front yard for all us students. Who could have known that Ray Trantham would later become a missionary to Ukraine, where he lived and worked for over 30 years?!

During our time in graduate school at Cincinnati Christian University we began to work with Team Expansion. We started to represent the missionaries in Uruguay and then Doug suggested that we should go on an internship to see the work in person, so that we could represent them better. Before going on the internship in the summer of 1984 I wanted to learn some Spanish. I used the language learning tapes that Doug Lucas had used when he was learning Spanish in Uruguay. We were following the LAMP principals (Language Acquisition Made Practical). The main idea is that you immerse yourself into the culture and mimic native speakers by repeating phrases that they record for you. In addition to my studies, I was also working at System Parking Garage in downtown Cincinnati. In the nighttime hours when we had some down time I would listen to the tapes and mimic the sounds, not knowing at all what the words meant. I just concentrated on getting the sounds right. One night, Becky and I went to eat supper with Doug and Penny, and I wanted to show them how much I had learned from the tapes. So, I said the phrase, *"Luisa es mi esposa."* Doug and Penny burst out in laughter, and I questioned, "What's wrong? Didn't I say it right?" Still laughing, Doug said, "No, you said it perfectly, but what you said was, 'Penny is my wife.'" Of course, we all had a good laugh over that one.

Uruguay and Costa Rica – 1984-1995

When we went to Uruguay for the internship it was Becky's first time to be on an overseas trip. We took a budget airline called Lineas Aereas Paraguayas (LAP). There was no leg room and it seemed like the passengers in front of us were in our LAP. Becky was very nervous, so when we began to take off, we prayed together and I read some scriptures. She held so tightly to my hand that my hand fell asleep. When we landed in Uruguay our missionary life began. We spent six weeks on that trip and I was completely convinced that mission work was for us and that we should return full time to work with the Team. When we returned home, we began to pray that if God wanted us to go to the mission field that He would provide support for us.

We had a great experience with the Wilmington (Ohio) Church of Christ who served as our "living link" support for 23 years. This congregation talked to Team Expansion to find a missionary to support and they helped link us together. Once we got connected with Wilmington, they provided financial support, leadership support, and emotional support for our family, both while we were on the mission field as well as when we came home on furlough after our terms on the field. The elders of the Wilmington Church provided great leadership and shepherding for our family. The ministers and staff participated in our ministry and especially in preparing for our furloughs back in the states. On two different occasions elders visited our mission work as well as the ministers. This congregation didn't just send us a check; they were our sending congregation in every sense of the word.

Before we went fulltime to the mission field, we spent six months living in Wilmington, and I was named the Minister of Missions on the church staff. There, we got to know the people and became a part of their lives. Then every time we would come home on furloughs, we would spend time with the congregation. They would always rent us a house and furnish it with donated furniture. Before we would come home, they would stock the pantry and refrigerator with food. They would prepare the house with the furniture that was donated for our stay, and they would make the beds and have everything ready for us when we arrived. I remember many times the church staff would meet us at the airport and take us to our new home, giving us the keys to the house, the church and the car. Wow...how they took care of us!

After our six months in Wilmington, we went off to San Jose, Costa Rica to learn Spanish. The language school connected us with a Costa Rican family who spoke no English so we were thrown into full immersion program of language learning. The family was polite and their house was modest but nice. There were some differences though. In this warm climate every night we had visitors to our room, the kind of visitors that crawl on four legs. If I had to get up at night to go the bathroom, we would turn on the light and start swatting the roaches with my flip flops. I'd kill a couple of them and the rest would scatter, then I would get up and go to the bathroom. After a couple of months there, we moved into our own apartment. We spent 10 months there in Costa Rica and our first daughter, Carol Marie, was born there. The girl who used to come and clean the house where we were staying, Julia, later became a Christian, and is still a good friend to our family to this day. We learned Spanish and enjoyed the culture. Then, we were ready for our service in Uruguay.

Once we moved to Uruguay, we joined the Team Expansion workers there to help start some churches. I had the pleasure of working with Larry Griffin in helping to start a church and preschool in the area of Montevideo known as *"Aires Puros,"* which means Pure Air. Perhaps this title originally was an appropriate name for a beautiful area of town along a peaceful river valley. However, in the time that we lived there, the riverbank and valley had turned into a slum area filled with shacks. The people who lived there made their money by rummaging through the trash that others threw out in order to find recyclable items. After they took out the items of paper, glass, and plastic, the rest of the trash was thrown out along the riverbank or in the river. The smell of that slum was notoriously bad, so the name *"Aires Puros"* turned out to be a satirical commentary on the slum area.

Larry Griffin had the desire to reach out to these poor people, so we decided to walk through the slum from time to time to meet people and find out what their needs were. The people seemed to be okay with living there in the slum and didn't seek anything for themselves, but they saw a great need for the children. The children needed to have an opportunity to learn and to get a good background before entering first grade in the public schools. We decided to start a preschool which was led by Ruth Griffin and her mother, Georgina Chicaguala, for 10 years. Through that ministry we saw many children transformed from slum dwellers into school kids who had hope, hygiene and education. We also started a church there because we knew that meeting spiritual needs had to go hand in hand with meeting physical needs. One of the teenagers who started coming to the church services there in Aires Puros was Daniel Raffo. Daniel and his cousin Edgar wanted to learn guitar. I was playing guitar for the worship services back then and offered to teach Daniel guitar if he would come an hour before the church services. He agreed, so I started teaching him the chords to play the worship choruses that we sang in church. Daniel had no rhythm and had little coordination in his hands to play the chords, but he had a strong desire to learn. Sometimes I felt it was a waste of time to struggle through those teaching sessions with Daniel, but we continued. We also taught Daniel the gospel. Somewhere along the way, Daniel gave his life to Christ and became a part of the church. We allowed him to play guitar along with me in the church services. It was a struggle for him as he missed the timing, and couldn't change chords at the right time, and it was also a struggle for those who listened! However, over time Daniel grew to be a fine young man and also a fine guitar player. God transformed his life and his guitar playing! He is now married and his whole family is part of the church in Montevideo. Daniel serves the church as a worship leader and an elder.

Miami and Cuba – 1996-2009

After we trained enough local leaders for the church in Uruguay the whole team moved to Miami, Florida to work with the Hispanic population there, and to make short term trips into Cuba. Over the 13 years that I lived in Miami, I made more than 33 trips to Cuba and along with other workers from Team Expansion, White Fields Evangelism, POEM and other ministries, helped start a house church movement that continues to grow throughout the island to this day. I have taken many others to Cuba with me to teach Bible and ministry courses to the preachers, and now there is a ministry school called Cuba Bible Institute that is located in Havana.

On one of these trips my Dad, Jack Bliffen, was with me and was teaching at the Institute. One late evening after a long day of teaching, Dad decided to go to bed early right after supper, and I decided to go for a walk along the coastline that was right down from the apartments that we were staying in. As I walked along the coast, the sun had recently set, and I was taking pictures, when just as I flashed a picture a military truck turned on the coastal road, and they saw me with my camera. I tried to ignore them and strolled on down the road looking out at the water, but after a few minutes they decided to come and question me. I heard the truck engine rev up and they came up the road right after me. Once they passed me, about five soldiers jumped out of the truck with weapons drawn and told me to stop, which I did. The first thing they did was ask me for my passport and visa (which was up in my room). They asked me where I was from, and what I was doing in Cuba. I said that I was from the United States and was touring the city and visiting some acquaintances. They wanted to see my passport and tourist visa, which I told them that I would be glad to go get from the apartment, but they would not let me leave. They would talk on the walkie talkie from time to time to their "Jefe" who said that he wanted to interview me. I said, just let me go get my passport and visa, and the whole matter would be resolved. They did not agree and would not let me go anywhere until the "Jefe" could get there to interview me. So, I waited for 20 minutes. The Jefe finally came, and he asked the same questions and I gave the same answers. He said that I was walking in a restricted area, which I didn't know. He said that many people had fled Cuba to leave for the north (the United States) from that coastline, and they wondered if I was part of a human smuggling ring. I said, oh no, that I was just walking along the coast enjoying the beautiful view and if you just let me get my passport all this would be resolved. He finally agreed and they put me in the truck and took me to the apartment that I was staying in. They loudly arrived at the apartment, and all the people from the apartments came out on the balconies and looked as I was ushered up to the door where I hurriedly got my passport and visa. Once I got the passport and visa, I returned to talk to the "Jefe" and he said that I was okay. They would not detain me any longer. He said, always keep your passport and visa with you, which I have faithfully done to this day! I finally got back to the apartment and showered and slept some. When I got up the next morning for breakfast, Dad was cheerful, and he asked how I was. I said, I didn't sleep very well, and I asked, didn't you hear any commotion last night? He said, no. He had slept through the whole ordeal! Anyway, I told him the whole story and we each kept our passport on us at all times for the rest of that trip, and every other trip!

Baptisms in Cuba were an adventure. Our very first trip to Cuba we had 6 baptisms. The first baptism was in a cove in Cojimar, where we later found out that Ernest Hemmingway had written his book "The Old Man and the Sea." Tanya Hernandez had accepted the gospel and we took her out to be baptized. We had to go at night, because the Cuban government persecuted Christians, and public baptisms were not allowed. I'll never forget that late night baptism in that cove. Tanya has remained a faithful Christian all these years, now living in Miami, FL. Other baptisms that week were held in a bathtub at a Christian's house in La Vibora. We have held baptisms in the sea, in bathtubs, and in rivers. One of the most unusual baptisms was held in a 50-gallon barrel of water. I stood outside the barrel, he got in, and I dunked him. Later on, we took portable baptistries from ARM ministries to be used by the churches. One trip we had baptisms at the church that meets on the flat roof over the preacher's house in el Sevillano. The preacher and other men took turns carrying buckets of water up to the roof to fill the ARM baptistry. My Dad and I both baptized men into Christ that day. It was a great day! Praise God for the hundreds of people baptized into Christ in Cuba through this church movement that has now spread all over Cuba!

Our ministry in Miami was beautiful for as long as it lasted. We had the joy of bringing many people to Christ in the Church which we called Iglesia Cristiana en West Kendall. We also trained a young man from our church to go to his home country of Ecuador as a missionary. He started a church there called Iglesia Cristiana en Cotacachi. In 2009 our ministry in Miami came to an end and we moved to Memphis. The church in Miami later merged with the South Winds Christian Church which had helped us get started back in 1997.

Memphis 2009-2021

We joined the staff of Mid-South Christian College in August 2009, being united once again with Larry Griffin, Jorge Chicaguala, and Greg Waddell from our Uruguay team. MSCC is a unique Bible college in that the same degrees that are offered in English are also offered in Spanish. In fact, every class is offered in both languages. We have accredited degrees in Ministry, Christian Education, and other practical degrees through cooperative programs with other Universities. It's been a joy to return to the college that I graduated from and to serve on this faculty and in partnership with mission minded professors and staff members. Every time that Larry and I get together for a meeting we say that we're having a class reunion since he and I were the only graduates in the BA program of MSCC in 1981. He was the Valedictorian and I was Salutatorian. I was second in my class but was also in the bottom half of the class. These are the joys of a small college.

While working at MSCC we have also served our local church East Win Christian Church in different ways. In 2012 we helped start a Hispanic congregation there which is currently being led by one of our Hispanic graduates from MSCC.

Granada, Spain 2017-2019

At Mid-South Christian College, I teach a Missions course which keeps my interest peaked for missions. Even back in 2009, when we first left Miami, we had been presented with the need of the mission work in Spain, and we even tried to recruit several workers for the work there. Through all of this we eventually decided to move to Spain following God's call to serve the least reached Spanish speaking nation.

Spain was very different from the Latin American countries where we had lived and worked. There were cultural differences, language differences, and the people in Spain are typically more resistant to the studying the Bible or hearing the gospel. Most Spanish people consider themselves Catholic even though they may not actually practice Catholicism or even believe in God. They don't want to change and are very skeptical of Evangelical Christianity, thinking that it is a foreign religion. Though we felt this resistance at almost every turn, we also were encouraged that a few Bible study groups were formed while we were there, and a few believers began meeting in a small church in Ogijares. We thank God for the team that continues the growing work there under the leadership of Gabo and Barbara Ayala.

One of the differences in Spain was the jet lag involved in travel across 7 time zones to get there. It would always take me several days to recover after one of those trans-Atlantic trips. In the year 2019 I had to make several trips back and forth from Spain to Memphis. On one occasion I had arrived just in time to meet another mission trip team coming from a supporting church in Florida. I remember trying to do all the tricks to avoid jet lag. I did not nap during the day and stayed awake until 10:00 and was just getting to a deep sleep when I was awakened by loud explosions outside the window. I woke up startled, rolled out of the bed and stumbled down the stairs. I could not remember where I was and all I could do was just wonder who was shooting missiles at us. It took a few minutes for me to realize that it was fireworks from the celebration of the town's festival. Those fireworks lasted till 2 am, and I didn't get any sleep that night. So, the next day I met the team and was busy that whole day. By the end of that day, I was exhausted and went to sleep early, about 10 pm. Once again, I woke up in the middle of the night, rolled out of bed and stumbled down the stairs. All I could think of was where was the baby. Maybe it was the thought of our one-year-old granddaughter, or the new baby of our team- mates. I didn't know which baby; I just knew that I was supposed to be taking care of some baby. Well, after a few minutes I realized where I was and that I was not taking care of any baby at that time. Still, I couldn't go back to sleep that night either. Jet lag is real!!

Mid-South Hispanic Ministry 2019-present

Upon returning from Spain and moving back to Memphis I was approached by Lynn Cook, the director of Arkansas Church Planting Network (ACPN). The Network had a desire to plant Hispanic Churches in Arkansas and they asked me to help coordinate those efforts. I was to recruit the church planters and help in training and coaching them through their beginning stages. This allows me to continue our mission efforts in Hispanic ministry while returning to serve at Mid-South Christian College as well. I officially began in January 2020. Our first church planter, David Mejia, moved to Little Rock in June 2020 and began Comunidad Cristiana in January 2021. Currently ACPN has approved two other church planters for two more cities in Arkansas. It is a change of pace for me to be mentoring young church planters, but for this stage of life it is a good change, and it looks like some great things are possible for the work of the Lord.

Reflecting back on how God has blessed us through the years, and how he has worked in and through our lives, we can truly say that He has been faithful! Thank God for the opportunity to serve Him in so many ways in so many places. To God be the glory!

E.W. and Mary Damron

Chapter 15

ELBERT WRIGHT AND MARY DAMRON

BY JERRY AND SHEILA BLIFFEN

Although this book is about the Bliffen family legacy, my in-laws are a big part of my story and I feel led to include them in this book. Elbert Wright Damron was born March 25, 1925 in Kenova, West Virginia, the youngest of five children born to Jerome R. and Cora Damron. E.W. got his name from his 2 grandfathers, Elbert Spurlock Belcher and Wright Damron. Wright Damron was born in 1840 and served on both sides in the Civil War. He first served in the Confederate Army in Pike County, enlisting with Regiment 5, Company G, on November 9, 1861 near Pound Gap. He could have been with the Rebels that were driven out of Pike County by James A. Garfield's Union Army March 16, 1862. After this event, Wright joined the 39th KY Infantry, Company B in Piketon (Pikeville), on November 14, 1862 to serve the rest of the war with the Union Army. I suppose he wanted to be on the winning side! He served with honor for over 2 years and died in 1910. His youngest son Jerome was born in 1887 and died in 1968. Wright and Jerome Damron are buried in Harold, Ky, where Sheila and I place flowers on their graves every May. Before their deaths, E.W. baptized both of his parents into Christ! Cora Damron is buried next to E.W. and Mary Damron at Johnson Memorial Cemetery in Pikeville.

Unfortunately, E.W.'s parents experienced marital problems and divorced when he was only four years old. For several months he and his siblings along with his mother went to live with his Grandmother Aurilla Damron, Wright's widow, at Betsy Layne, Kentucky. Elbert Belcher eventually offered a house to his daughter Cora in Belcher Bottom near Elkhorn City. She moved her children to this little house but there was never stability for the children after this move. E.W. spent time living with his brother, Gene, in Williamson, West Virginia, with his Uncle Anthony Damron in Harold, and summers with his Mom at Belcher. When living with his Uncle, he attended Betsy Layne School where he graduated from 8th grade and attended his freshman year before dropping out. He enjoyed having his own horse, Tarzan, which he could be seen riding all around the Harold community. Once he made wooden ice skates and skated from Harold to Pikeville (about 9 miles) and back on the frozen Big Sandy River!

On his 18th birthday, March 25, 1943, E.W. joined the United States Navy to serve his country in WWII. He was sent to the Pacific Theater where he served in Australia, the Solomon Islands, Papua New Guinea, and the Admiralty Islands. E.W. was a prop specialist for PBY airplanes. While serving on Manus Island, just north of Papua New Guinea, he witnessed the explosion of the ammunition ship Mount Hood on November 10, 1944. Over 350 men were killed in that tragic explosion. Many years later my brother Jim, would serve our Lord in the same area my father-in-law served our country, half-way around the world! E.W. was honorably discharged from the Navy on Nov. 7, 1945.

It was soon after he completed his military service that he met his future wife, Mary Bartley. She was selling tickets at the movie theater in Elkhorn City. He said he made several trips to buy popcorn so he could see the ticket girl. This was the beginning of a courtship that led to their marriage on November 29, 1948. In March of 1949, E.W. and Mary were baptized into Christ in the Russell Fork of the Big Sandy at Belcher, Kentucky. They had been invited to a revival at the Ferrells Creek Church of Christ by E.W.'s oldest sister Pauline, and this one act of encouragement led to E.W. and Mary's lifetime of service to Christ. The river had to be cold, but that didn't deter them from making this life-changing decision, being immersed by Preacher Kenis Hunt. Two of Preacher Hunt's sons, Orville and Dale Hunt, were members of the Coal Run Church during my ministry there. E.W. actually baptized these Hunt brothers.

During this same time frame in 1949 when E.W. was converted to Christ, my Dad was a student at Kentucky Christian College and preaching for the Coal Run Church of Christ. It didn't take E.W. long to begin preaching the gospel. He was a naturally gifted speaker. He began studying God's Word at home and loved sharing what he learned. When he first started preaching, he did not own an automobile, but his sister Pauline did! She told him to never turn down an opportunity to preach, he could use her car to go wherever God led him. And that's what he did.

On January 7, 1954 E.W. and Mary's home was blessed with a baby girl, Sheila. Seven months later, in July, E.W. was invited to preach a revival at Coal Run. It lasted three weeks, with 26 additions to the little congregation that met on the hill at the mouth of Stone Coal. The church needed a full-time preacher, so that fall, E.W. rented out his Texaco Service Station at Belcher and answered the call to become the first full-time minister in the history of the Coal Run Church of Christ. Later the highway bought the service station building from him. The church was unable to pay E.W. enough to live on, so he and Mary used the money from the rent of his service station building to supplement his salary from the church. E.W. traveled from Pikeville to Grundy one or two nights a week for several years, studying at Grundy Bible Institute under Bible teachers like Clarence Greenleaf, Paul Bennett, Bill Morgan, and Clinton Looney. Though he never graduated from high school, E.W. had a sharp mind, which he used to learn God's Word. He had a great ability to memorize scripture and could preach for 30-45 minutes with very few notes and little reading ... most of his messages came from his memorization and living out what he preached.

In 1962, after helping to build a new building at Coal Run, E.W. was called to minister to the Elkhorn City Church of Christ, very near his home community of Belcher. He enjoyed a successful 2 ½ year ministry at Elkhorn City. Sheila has many fond memories of those years, having made good friends in the church and the community. Just recently, I did some supply preaching for the Elkhorn City Church of Christ.

The Poplar Creek Church of Christ in Buchanan County approached E.W. in 1966 about accepting the call to minister to their congregation. He accepted and moved his family to Poplar Creek and served the Lord there until the end of 1968. During his years at Poplar Creek the church grew as E.W. baptized many people into Christ. His personality was such that he never met a stranger. He had the ability to meet people where they were and make friends, all the while encouraging them to a new life in Christ. He witnessed to people while fishing, squirrel hunting, and playing golf. The people at Poplar Creek loved the Damron family and showed it in so many ways. It was a sad time when he resigned, as they had many, many genuine friends in that community and church family.

In January of 1969, E.W. answered the call of God on his life to return to serve the Coal Run congregation that he loved so much. He served in this return ministry with great success until his retirement in June of 1990 at the age of 65.

During his years in ministry, E.W. preached countless revival meetings in nine different states. Many churches invited him back multiple times. Preaching revivals was one of his great loves, but he was always ready to come back home to Mary and Sheila and his located ministry. Hundreds of people came to Christ during E.W.'s many years of ministry.

Grundy Bible Institute had been a huge blessing to E.W. in studying God's Word and preparing him for greater service in the Kingdom, and it was his desire to have a Bible Institute, training Christians in Kentucky. In September of 1969, he led the Coal Run leaders to establish East Kentucky Bible Institute. In the beginning years, all classes were held at the Coal Run building two nights a week. Different area preachers taught the classes as had been the case at GBI. But because Pike County is such a large county and the churches were spread apart by many miles, it was decided that classes would be taught in the different congregations. For many years six different Churches of Christ throughout eastern Kentucky hosted classes in their buildings. EKBI has been a great teaching arm of the church for over 50 years.

When the Pike County and Buchanan County Churches of Christ worked together to purchase land and establish the Church of Christ Youth Camp on Baldwin Mountain, E.W. was one of the first Deans in 1969. He and Jim Viers worked together to lead a Senior Week with over 100 campers and a Junior week with a huge number of children attending that first year. Sheila was a camper in the first Senior week and a team leader in the first Junior week. CCYC was always an important part of Sheila's life, as well as her parents. E.W. continued working as Dean, Assistant Dean, Vesper Speaker, Teacher and whatever else he was needed to do at CCYC for many years. Mary was right there with him as Dorm Mother, Team Leader and helper in the kitchen. Sheila continued this tradition as my wife, helping me in many, many weeks of camp. After our daughters came along, they loved attending CCYC and eventually both became great camp workers. Our daughter, Sarah was actually employed by the camp for two summers while she was a college student. The Church of Christ Youth Camp was blessed to have men like E.W., Jim Viers, Clarence Greenleaf, Mike Trent, Bob Werntz and Bill Ford to set the pace for many years of teaching God's Word on the mountain. One of E.W.'s favorite times each year was attending the National Prayer Clinic in October. He preached, presided, and encouraged many, many wonderful men of God who gathered on the mountain of prayer year after year. He passed away just a couple of weeks after attending the Prayer Clinic in 2009.

It was on a Monday night, October 25, 2009... E.W. was a student, attending an East Kentucky Bible Institute class at Coal Run, when his hand became numb at the end of class. Very soon after he went home, he called and let us know he needed to go to the Emergency Room. Sheila and I took him, and he was immediately diagnosed with a blood clot in his neck. He was administered medication to dissolve the blood clot, but it caused a brain bleed that led to his death the following morning. His death was so sudden and such a shock, but in hindsight, I know it was a great blessing that he didn't have to suffer long. Mary was confined to a wheelchair, and overnight, Sheila and I assumed the responsibility of her primary care givers. Mary had been an excellent support for E.W. throughout all of his years in ministry, and a wonderful mother to Sheila. On March 26, 2014, Mary went home to be with the Lord under very similar circumstances as E.W., suffering a stroke.

The lives of E.W. and Mary have had a tremendous impact on me and thousands of others across the country. They too, have a wonderful legacy of faith!

Chapter 16

A Brief History of Vansant and Coal Run Churches of Christ
By Jerry Bliffen

Vansant Church of Christ

The Vansant Church of Christ was founded by members from the Grundy Church of Christ in 1957. It started in the home of George and Marie Looney, parents of Ann Deel. Property was soon purchased from the Looneys by the Grundy Church (later paid back by the Vansant Church), where the church building was constructed. That same year, the Poplar Creek Church of Christ was also started by the Grundy church. Preacher Clarence Greenleaf did not want to have a mega-church in downtown Grundy, but rather wanted Churches of Christ scattered throughout communities all over Buchanan County.

The first minister of the Vansant Church of Christ was Burb Rife. After about a year or so, he was followed by brother Clinton Looney. Clinton was converted to Christ at the Grundy Church of Christ and in my opinion became one of the most effective evangelists and missionaries in our entire brotherhood! In 1961, he was teaching missions at Grundy Bible Institute when both he and Bill Morgan, minister of the Haysi Church of Christ, decided to go to the Mexican mission field. Bill had attended public school and four years at Kentucky Christian College with my Dad. He and Clinton had worked together in various churches in southwest Virginia. Bill also held revivals at Coal Run where E.W. was ministering, and years later led a sight-seeing trip to Mexico for the Damrons and others from Coal Run. Clinton, his wife Melba, and their four children drove all the way to Mexico City to begin Looney Mexico Mission that continues to this day. Literally thousands of people have been converted to Christ, and hundreds of churches, camps, and other Christian institutions have been established throughout the nation of Mexico through his influence. I have been blessed to be with Clinton on many occasions in both the Appalachian Mountains and the beautiful mountains and plains of Mexico. I have witnessed his pulpit ministry as well as his personal, one-on-one, evangelistic effectiveness! I put Clinton Looney in the same category as Sam Hurley, the founder of Mountain Mission School, which has literally provided for thousands of orphans and needy children from around the world. They are two amazing mountaineer men of God! The question was once asked about Jesus, "Can any good thing come out of Nazareth?" Someone might question, "Can any good thing come out of Grundy?" I, along with thousands of others, can attest to the fact that a lot of good has come out of Grundy! And through the years, hundreds of thousands of dollars have come out of the Grundy area to the support of Looney Mexico Mission and Mountain Mission School! The beginning of Looney Mexico Mission came from the Grundy and Vansant Churches of Christ. Mary Cook of the Vansant Church has been the forwarding agent for Looney Mexico Mission since its beginning, serving now for 60 years! Praise God for the influence of the Buchanan County Churches of Christ in this great work for Christ.

After Clinton Looney went to Mexico, Harry Welch ministered at Vansant for a short time, followed by Jackie Miller, in 1962. Under Jackie's leadership the church began a bus ministry and purchased property next to their existing building from Frank Bevins of the Grundy Church. Jackie even purchased a Volkswagen bus for his wife Pattie to pick up children and bring to church. Jackie, Bob McAllister, and Emory Brown met with the owner of property on top of Baldwin Mountain and arranged the purchase of that land which would become the Church of Christ Youth Camp. The camp property was purchased for $3,500 -- a great investment for the Kingdom's work! Jackie had a tremendous ministry at Vansant, living with his family in an apartment in back of the church building. The first wedding he performed was Jerry and Betty Shields. Jerry later became an elder and Betty was the teacher for the Ladies Sunday School class for many years. Jackie organized a youth singing group, "The Heavenly Harmonettes," who sang many Saturdays on the daily radio program for the Churches of Christ on WNRG. Vacation Bible School weeks would have 200 in attendance!

Jackie also had a strong influence on Jim Hill entering the ministry. Jim followed Jackie as the next minister at Vansant around 1966. The church continued to grow under the ministry of Brother Jim. They started the weekly television program "What Does the Bible Plainly Say?" in the early 1970's. Jim left the Vansant church in January,1976.

David McVeigh became the interim minister for six months at Vansant, beginning in January of 1976. On July 4, 1976, I began my ministry at Vansant where I served for 14 years until July 1, 1990. Mike Rife followed me and has served his home church for the past 31 years! Under Mike's ministry, the church has thrived and seen tremendous growth. Property has been purchased on both sides of the building and presently the church has two Sunday morning services.

The Vansant church has been very involved in the Church of Christ Youth Camp since its beginning in 1969 -- clearing the land, with elder Henry Deel doing a lot of dozer work. Vansant members helped build the buildings, and many volunteers worked in the kitchen every summer! The outstanding camp manager for over thirty years was Larry Fields, a deacon in the Vansant Church. He sacrificed more than any other human to see that camp weeks ran smoothly and the buildings and grounds were kept in excellent shape. Larry's mother-in-law, Polly Kennedy, wife of Bill Kennedy, another deacon at Vansant, served as the camp cook for many years beginning in 1990. She was an excellent cook and Bill helped clean and carry out trash for many years, though he really wasn't able. Many weeks of camp have had other Vansant members serve as dorm parents, teachers, team leaders, deans and cooks. Vansant has also been a very missions-minded church, even giving its best church van to a mission in need in New York City back in the 80's. In spite of poor economic conditions, and the constant moving away of people from Buchanan County to the Abingdon, Virginia area and other places, the Vansant church continues to thrive!

Coal Run Church of Christ

In the late 1800's, evangelist Robert Burns Neal, was living in Grayson, Kentucky. (Neal was instrumental in the founding of Christian Normal Institute in 1919. Christian Normal Institute became Kentucky Christian College in the fall of 1944. The girl's dorm was named for him - "Neal Hall.") In addition to being an educator, brother Neal's primary work was that of an evangelist and church planter. He rode his horse, Daisy, up and down the Big Sandy River preaching and establishing churches in many communities. Two of those communities were Coal Run and Pikeville. Brother Neal held church services in the Coal Run grade school building located on a hill near the mouth of Stone Coal creek. A small group of people would assemble to hear him preach and became interested in erecting a church building. The Pike County Board of Education had plans to build a new school building at another location, so with the help of Betty Weddington, a tract of land was deeded to the Coal Run Church of Christ. The church building was completed in the summer of 1908 and was dedicated with about 150 people attending. A church bell was hung in the belfry that had once been on the "Andy Hatcher" steamboat that had traveled up and down the Big Sandy River before there were many roads or a railroad. The Andy Hatcher was a 3-story steamboat built in Charleston, West Virginia in 1889. The boat was destroyed by fire in a Paintsville, Kentucky harbor on Christmas night,1897. Its bell, cast in Hillsboro, Ohio, was saved and used by the Paintsville Grade School until it was acquired by the Coal Run Church of Christ. The bell, now over 140 years old, is still used on occasion by the church to this day, where it has been housed in the church's sign on 149 Church Street. R.B. Neal became the minister of the Pikeville Christian Church from 1909-1912, during which time the church built its first building on Scott Avenue, a building that still stands today! In those days there was no division between the Christian Church and the Church of Christ, though the Christian Church in Pikeville later became a Disciples of Christ Christian Church.

About this time, Brother Tom Mead was holding church services at Coal Run once a month. They were not having Sunday school at this time, and church attendance was about 30. Through the years the church struggled with attendance, but revived somewhat under the ministry of S.C. Honeycutt, who preached for a number of years and baptized many people into Christ. The church was also served by student ministers from Kentucky Christian College, including Julian Hunt, Benny Hunt, and others. When Jack Bliffen came as a student minister in 1948, the church had few members, among whom were Minnie Weddington and Opal Mann. Mrs. Weddington had a large house near the Coal Run swinging bridge where my Dad would spend the night on Saturdays, after riding a bus up old US 23 from Ashland. He remembers getting sick on the bus ride many times. In the early 50s, Brother Lee Ford, owner and operator of a shoe repair shop in Pikeville, came and held services twice a month, and the church attendance began to increase. E.W. Damron of Belcher, Kentucky was invited to preach a revival in July of 1954. The revival lasted three weeks and 26 people responded by baptism or rededication. At that time, the church saw the need for a full-time minister, and E.W. began his ministry at Coal Run, serving as the church's first full-time evangelist, in the fall of 1954. He rented out his Texaco business at Belcher and moved to Coal Run. According to an article in "The Mountain Evangelist", published by the Grundy Church of Christ in November 1956, the church grew in two years with 80 new members, and an average attendance of 160! It was a common sight to see the Coal Run congregation heading to the river for baptisms.

The C&O Railroad Company purchased the property where the original church building was located, and the church needed to move and construct a new building. Property was purchased where the building presently stands. The building committee consisted of Opal Mann, E.W. Damron, and Roscoe Gillam. On April 9, 1961 ground was broken and construction began shortly thereafter. Many hours of hard labor were donated by the men of the church as well as friends in the community. E.W. and his father, Jerome Damron, laid the blocks for the new building. A dedication service was held on October 28, 1962 in the new building with approximately 400 people in attendance!

In 1963, E.W. left Coal Run and went to minister at the Elkhorn City Church of Christ. Brother Larry Ogden came to Coal Run as the new minister. He concluded his ministry in August,1966. In April,1967, Brother Eugene McGee came to serve as the next minister. His work continued through August 1968. In the fall of 1968, the officers of the church approached brother E.W. about returning to minister at Coal Run again. At that time, he was preaching for the Poplar Creek Church of Christ, near Grundy, Virginia. E.W. agreed to return and began his second ministry at Coal Run on January 1, 1969.

In the fall of 1969, East Kentucky Bible Institute began at Coal Run under the leadership of Brother Damron. Its' purpose was to train church leaders, or anyone wanting to know more about God's word. Through the years, classes met on weeknights at different church buildings throughout Pike county.

In 1970, the Highway Department was building a new four-lane highway through Coal Run for US 23. Because of the new highway buying properties, the church was able to purchase a three-bedroom brick home for $4000 and move it to a location behind the church building for another $4000. This became the church's parsonage where the Damrons, and later Sheila and I lived while ministering there. In 1975, the church had a note burning signifying that all indebtedness for the church building and parsonage was paid.

In 1975, I was a student at KCC and son-in-law to E.W. The elders called me to serve as the church's first youth minister. I served in this position until July,1976 when I accepted the call to preach for the Vansant Church of Christ. Other youth ministers through the years included Jeff Stanley, John

Gasser, Keith Sergent, Jordan Stanley, Aaron Davis, and Nathan Mills. The 70's and 80's were good years at the Coal Run Church of Christ, with the church enjoying steady growth. In 1990, E.W. retired from full-time ministry at the age of 65. In his two terms of service at Coal Run, he had been the minister for about 29 years.

My first Sunday at Coal Run was July 1, 1990. Sheila, Bethany, Sarah, and I transferred our membership from Vansant to Coal Run that day. The church continued to enjoy steady growth, and in 1994 purchased the Russell Tackett property on the west side of our property. The Tackett house became a Youth Center that was used on Sundays and Wednesdays for several years for youth classes. The front and side yard of the Tackett house gave us some much-needed additional parking, and the backyard soon became a basketball court for the youth and the preacher!

In 1998, the church totally remodeled the auditorium, and opened the balcony to seat an additional 45 people. That was also the year we purchased the Homer Edmonds' property on the east side of our building. In 2002, the church purchased the property of Lucille Ratliff, also on the east side of the building to give us ample room to construct a new auditorium. We also began a building fund which grew to $800,000 when we broke ground on May 31, 2009 for our new building. The elders appointed a building committee, five men and five ladies, and hired Steve Treap as the Construction Manager. He worked closely with the committee to construct the new building and remodel the old building.

August 15, 2010 was the first Sunday in our new auditorium. Attendance that day was 309 with two baptisms, one rededication, and one transfer of membership. A special dedication service was held on August 29 with over 300 people in attendance. God provided for the church in amazing ways, so that the church was able to become debt free in one year, burning our note on August 14, 2011! The church then began remodeling the old building and started a preschool ministry, "Kingdom Kids" in 2013. In 2014, the church purchased additional property on its west side from Danny Hurt. The church plans use this property for a Family Life Center and currently has started a building fund for that construction project. So, from 1994 until 2014 the church purchased 4 properties and constructed a $1.5 million church building and is totally debt-free. To God be the glory, great things He has done!

From 2002 until 2011, the church presented a Live Nativity twice every December that was attended by many in the community. One year we had four performances, two on Saturday evening and two on Sunday evening. Between 300 and 400 people would attend these live presentations of the birth of Christ. My wife Sheila directed the Nativities, and many people in our church family worked tirelessly in various ways to present these programs. Through the years, we actually built two different stables on our property down near the Big Sandy River! The Live Nativity was always a very time-consuming and difficult effort with uncertain weather conditions, but pales in comparison to what Mary and Joseph endured over 2000 years ago!

Throughout the years the Coal Run Church has had a very dynamic mission outreach. In addition to sponsoring many short-term mission trips, the church has supported other churches in the area, a food ministry called HOPE, in which we give out food nearly every month, International Disaster Emergency Services, Westcare Homeless Shelter, Appalachian Pregnancy Care Center, three missions in Mexico, missions in Haiti, Jamaica, Spain, two missions in India, Papua New Guinea, Africa, a radio and TV ministry, a Braille ministry, Bible Colleges, Mountain Mission School, Church of Christ Youth Camp, VA/WV Evangelism, Diamond Willow Ministries, and others as needs arise. Only God knows what has been accomplished for the expansion of the Kingdom of God through these efforts!

In July 2020, I retired from 44 years of full-time ministry, 30 of which were at Coal Run. Trey Mouton was hired as our new minister and continues in that position today. At this writing, the Covid-19 virus has affected the church in some negative ways, but the Lord's work goes on. Thank God for His continued blessings on the Coal Run Church of Christ!

CPSIA information can be obtained
at www.ICGtesting.com
Printed in the USA
LVHW011542050422
715339LV00010B/710